Jewish-
Christian
Relations
in
Today's World

Jewish-Christian Relations in Today's World

Edited by
James E. Wood, Jr.

THE MARKHAM PRESS FUND OF
BAYLOR UNIVERSITY PRESS

Waco, Texas 1971

JEWISH-CHRISTIAN RELATIONS IN TODAY'S WORLD

PREFACE

With the exception of Franklin H. Littell's *"Kirchenkampf and Holocaust: The German Church Struggle and Nazi Anti-Semitism in Retrospect"* and "Have Jews and Christians a Common Future?" all the articles in this volume were originally presented at the Symposium on Jewish-Christian Relations and Education at Baylor University, 24-26 January 1971, sponsored by the J. M. Dawson Studies in Church and State of Baylor University and the Anti-Defamation League of B'nai B'rith. The Symposium, which brought together scholars from eighteen different universities and theological schools, was specifically addressed to "making available scholarly interpretations on matters of common concern to Jews and Christians" and "to furthering Jewish-Christian understanding through academic channels of teaching and research." Aspects of historical and contemporary Jewish thought and culture as well as current concerns in Jewish-Christian relationships were explored. The expressed purpose of the Symposium was to make available to college and seminary faculties current interpretations of Jews, Judaism, and Jewish-Christian relations and to stimulate more effective integration of Judaic Studies and Jewish-Christian history within existing programs of higher education, and perhaps stimulate new course offerings.

These articles are now presented in this publication as a part of the ongoing Jewish-Christian dialogue which, when authentic and honest, is essential not only for some measure of restitution and resolution of the Jewish-Christian conflict which has so marred Western history, more specifically Western Christianity, but ultimately for rediscovery and reaffirmation of authentic, meaningful Jewish-Christian relations.

Special acknowledgment must be made to the Anti-Defamation League of B'nai B'rith and the J. M. Dawson Studies in Church and State for their joint sponsorship of the Symposium on Jewish-Christian Relations and Education. The editor is profoundly grateful to the authors of the essays in this volume and also to Mr. Joseph S. Gordesky, Southwest Director of the Anti-Defamation League, who collaborated with the editor as coordinator of the Symposium. Sincere appreciation must also be expressed to all of the participants in the Symposium, representing various universities and theological schools, and to my colleagues at Baylor University who shared in multiple ways the responsibility for hosting the Symposium and presiding during its sessions —in particular Robert T. Miller, Bob E. Patterson, Rufus B. Spain, and William G. Toland. A particular debt is owed Dr. Solomon S. Bernards, ADL Director of Interreligious Cooperation, not only for his frequent counsel in the planning of the Symposium and his significant contribution to the Symposium program itself in leading workshop sessions, but also for his valuable assistance in the preparation of this volume for final publication.

———————

This volume is published by the Markham Press Fund of Baylor University Press, established in memory of Dr. L. N. and Princess Finch Markham of Longview, Texas, by their daughters Mrs. R. Matt Dawson of Corsicana, Texas, and Mrs. B. Reid Clanton of Longview, Texas.

James E. Wood, Jr.

Baylor University

1 October 1971

CONTENTS

INTRODUCTION

Jewish–Christian Relations in Historical Perspective

Jewish-Christian relations occupy an integral place in both the history of Judaism and the history of Christianity. Much of the history of Judaism is characterized by reflection on the anguish of living and concern for survival in the midst of a Christian dominated world which came to be known as Christendom. So far as Christian history is concerned, there can be no true history of Christianity without major reference to Judaism and Jewish-Christian relations. Likewise, no history of church-state relations and religious liberty in the Western world can be written without special attention being given to Jewish-Christian relations and the status of Jews in Christian Europe.

The juxtaposition of Judaism and Christianity offers in some ways a strange paradox in the history of religion. On the one hand, no two faiths are more deeply rooted in a common historical source, and, on the other hand, between no two faiths have there been greater misunderstandings, greater hostilities, and more open conflicts. Unfortunately, conflict and not concord has been the hallmark throughout most of the history of Jewish-Christian relations. It is no exaggeration to say that the supreme tragedy of Christian history is that Christian anti-Semitism, sustained by theological foundations, has had such a long and persistent place in so much of Christian history. Indeed, the saddest part of this tragedy of human history is that Christian anti-Semitism is not yet ended, nor even formally disavowed in much of contemporary Christianity.

Admittedly, anti-Semitism is deeply and peculiarly rooted in Christianity, both in its theology and in its history. No amount of qualifying or rationalizing can alter the basic contention of numerous Jewish and Christian scholars alike that anti-Semitism is inextricably intertwined with empirical Christianity. Furthermore, these attitudes and practices from the past still cast their shadows over the present in Jewish-Christian relations. Charles Y. Glock and Rodney Stark in their sobering sociological analysis, *Christian Beliefs and Anti-Semitism,* based upon a study conducted by the University of California Research Center, found that "only 5 percent of Americans with anti-Semitic views lack all rudiments of a religious basis for their prejudice" and that "religion actually operated to produce anti-Semitism." Such studies in recent years have all too painfully served to confirm that the primary and ultimate cause of anti-Semitism, which has infected so much of Western history, is a religious one with roots going back through many centuries even to early Christianity.

I

The history of Christianity does not begin with the first century A.D., but with Biblical Judaism. The tragedy of Christian anti-Semitism stems in part, at least, from its failure or refusal to recognize that Christianity is historically rooted in Biblical Judaism. The Jewishness of Jesus and New Testament Christianity needs continually to be reaffirmed. It must always be remembered that Jesus was a Jew (a "star out of Jacob"), and a faithful one, throughout his life in Palestine. He upheld the Torah, and his own teachings were essentially and radically Jewish. Jesus reaffirmed, as a Jew, that the command in Deuteronomy 6:5, "Thou shalt love the Lord thy God with all thy heart, and with all thy soul, and with all thy mind," is "the first and greatest commandment" (Matt. 22:37-38). "And the second," Jesus declared, "is like unto it, Thou shalt love thy neighbour as thyself" (Matt. 22:39), which he quoted also from the Torah, Leviticus 19:18. "On these two commandments," Jesus affirmed, "hang all the law and the prophets" (Matt. 22:40). Jesus' religious language, his parables, his poetic and prophetic sayings, and his prayers were all unmistakably Jewish. His message, the Kingdom of God, was a Jewish concept which had already become integral to the prophetic tradition of Israel. The parallels to Jesus' teachings in Jewish literature prior to the first century abound, including much of the Sermon on the Mount of Matthew 5-7. The Lord's Prayer itself may be traced to Jewish sources. While Jesus left his unmistakable stamp upon these Jewish teachings by means of the interpretations, the Jewishness of Jesus is undeniable. As James Parkes observed in

Judaism and Christianity, the teachings of Jesus presuppose a Jewish environment and it is impossible to imagine their having come out of any other milieu.

Jewish historians and theologians alike, particularly since the nineteenth century, have recognized the Jewishness of Jesus, while many of the early Church Fathers, as with many subsequent Catholic and Protestant theologians, have ignored and even categorically denied the Jewishness of Jesus. Although the Christian Christ has remained unacceptable to contemporary Judaism, the Jewish Jesus has often been appealing to manifestly devout Jewish thinkers and theologians. One of modern Judaism's greatest theologians, the late Martin Buber, wrote poignantly of his view of Jesus in a volume entitled, *Two Types of Faith,* as follows: "From my youth onwards I have found in Jesus my great brother. . . . My own fraternally open relationship to him has grown ever stronger and clearer, and today I see him more strongly and clearly than before." Acceptance of the historical Jesus, even as the Messiah, has not been regarded, either in the first century or the twentieth century, as necessarily a repudiation of one's Jewish faith.

The matrix of Christianity was Jewish, and, for Jewish thinkers at least, Christianity has been rightly regarded, in a profound sense, as the daughter of Judaism. The twelve apostles were Jewish, nearly all of the followers of Jesus were Jewish, those who wept over his crucifixion by Roman soldiers were Jewish, and those who first carried the Christian Gospel to the world beyond Palestine were Jewish. The Christian Gospel was first preached, in Palestine as well as in Asia Minor, in the synagogues. Paul, the greatest interpreter of Christianity and its leading missionary during the first century, never ceased to regard himself as a Jew: "I myself am an Israelite, a descendant of Abraham, a member of the tribe of Benjamin" (Rom. 11:1). The Scriptures, as well as most of the rites and symbols, of the early church were Jewish. Every aspect of the original apostolic proclamation was supported by an appeal to the Jewish Scriptures. The preaching of the apostles was first addressed to the Jews and expressed in Jewish theological terms. Among the earliest Christian writings are those of unmistakable Jewish character, written by Jewish believers, such as *Testaments of the Twelve Patriarchs, Psalms of Solomon, Apocalypse of James, Apocalypse of Peter,* and *Epistle of the Eleven Apostles.* Some of these early Christian writings, such as the *Testaments of the Twelve Patriarchs*, were little more than a Christian revision of Jewish writings. The New Testament itself is preeminently a collection of the writings of Jewish Christians, and the Jewish Scriptures remain indispensable to the study and the interpretation of the New Testament; indeed, the Jewish Scriptures are presupposed throughout the New Testament.

To the outside world, there was no real distinction between Judaism and Christianity before the end of the first century. For example, Suetonius and Tacitus, Roman historians writing in the second century, still regarded Christianity as a Jewish sect. The simple fact is that Judeo-Christianity, comprised essentially of Jewish or "Torah-true" Christians (those who remained faithful to Jewish observances such as circumcision, the Sabbath, and Temple worship), was the dominant form of Christianity throughout the first century and almost to the middle of the second century. First under the leadership of James, the brother of Jesus, Judeo-Christianity was centered in Jerusalem until the city's destruction in A.D. 70. The leadership of the early church was predominantly Jewish. Eusebius, the father of Christian ecclesiastical history, early in the fourth century quoted from Hegesippus that "those who were called the brothers of the Saviour governed the entire church, in virtue of their being martyrs and relatives of the Lord." Again in his *Ecclesiastical History*, Eusebius wrote, "I have learned from written documents that, until the siege of the Jews under Hadrian, there had been in Jerusalem a succession of fifteen bishops, all of whom are said to have been Hebrews of ancient stock. In fact, the entire church of Jerusalem consisted at that time of practicing Hebrews." Judeo-Christianity was identified as "the church of the circumcision" and its leaders referred to as "the bishops of the circumcision." Not only in Jerusalem and in Palestine but throughout the Mediterranean world, including Rome itself, the earliest Christian communities consisted of Judeo-Christians. Until the second century only a small minority of the Christian community was comprised of those from the pagan or Gentile world. Fortunately, the Jewishness of Jesus and early Christianity is being rediscovered today at a time when the need for Jewish-Christian dialogue was never greater. As Jean Cardinal Daniélou has observed, "The recovery of this Jewish Christianity is one of the achievements of recent scholarship."

II

As the Jewishness of early Christianity is undeniable, so is the conflict between Judaism and early Christianity clearly evident. As has already been indicated, there is no reason for not viewing Jesus as a faithful Jew, for certainly he so regarded himself. Nevertheless, as James Parkes observed in *The Conflict of the Church and the Synagogue,* "The origin of the profound difference which exists between Judaism and Christianity must ultimately be related to the teaching of Jesus, although He Himself lived and died a Jew." While Jesus wanted to bring about reforms in contemporary Judaism, at no time did he abandon Judaism itself. Clearly, Jesus did experience as a prophet opposition from certain priests and Pharisees because of his attitude toward and interpretation of Halachah, i.e., the entire body of oral and written Jewish law and tradition. Jesus refused to give to these traditions the force of Torah itself. Furthermore, Jesus, as later would Paul, could not accept the primacy or the adequacy of Torah. After Jesus' crucifixion, many Jews saw the status of Torah as the supreme authority threatened also by the Christian claim that Christ, not Torah, represented "the way, the truth, and the life." The unorthodox view of Jesus and his followers concerning Torah inevitably provoked conflict between Judaism and Christianity. From his own extensive study of Jewish-Christian relations, Parkes concluded that "it was the Law and not the Crucifixion which was the basis of this separation" which resulted between Judaism and Christianity. During the latter part of the first century, Diaspora Jews, living as they did in a Gentile world, felt more resentful of and more threatened by Christianity's view of the Law than did the Palestinian Jews. Stephen and Paul, for example, aroused far greater hostility from among the Jews of the Diaspora than from among the Jews in Palestine. In part this was because Hellenistic Christianity outside of Palestine provoked far more hostility from the Jews of the Diaspora than did Palestinian Christianity among Palestinian Jews.

To be sure, the cleavage between Judaism and Christianity was also deepened by the claims of Christ's Deity, the acceptance of which was a Jewish impossibility. As indicated earlier, whether or not Jesus was the Messiah did not constitute in itself a basis for Christianity's separation from Judaism so far as Judaism was concerned, but the teaching of the early church concerning the Deity of Christ and the Incarnation was and remains to this day the great

theological divide between Judaism and Christianity. The Christological formulations offered by the early church further offended the
Jews who resented the fact that Jesus, a fellow-Jew, was declared to
be God, a declaration which outside of trinitarian theology could
only be interpreted as a direct violation of the First Commandment.
Meanwhile, the rejection by the Jewish community of these Christological affirmations of faith concerning Jesus represented to the
Christian community a direct repudiation of the central truth of the
Christian Gospel. To Rabbinic Judaism, to state it directly, the claim
of Christian "liberty" from the primacy of Torah could only be
interpreted as blasphemy, and the Jewish acceptance of the Christian
claims of Jesus as Christ and Lord could only mean apostasy.

Notwithstanding these conflicts, Christianity remained primarily a
sect within Judaism throughout the first century. Not until the
period between A.D. 70-140 did Christianity gradually become
separated from Judaism, but, even during this period, Judeo-
Christianity continued to remain dominant. Hellenistic Christianity,
comprised primarily of pagano-Christians and represented by Paul,
became a third force. Still, prior to A.D. 140, the church was
comprised mainly of Jews or proselytes converted to Judaism; only
after this time did converts to Christianity come mainly from among
the Gentiles. The earlier identification of Christianity with the
"church of the circumcision" gradually came to be transferred to the
"church of the Gentiles," as Gentile Christians came to be pre-
dominant over Jewish Christians in the Roman world. While Judeo-
Christianity continued to coexist within the whole of Christianity for
another several centuries, Jewish customs and rituals tended to be
regarded as incompatible with the Christian faith. The identification
of Christianity as a Jewish sect gradually became lost, and within a
few centuries Judeo-Christianity virtually disappeared. In becoming a
universal faith, a church of the Gentiles, Hellenistic Christianity
severed its ties with Judaism. The triumph of Hellenistic Christianity
over Judeo-Christianity is reflected in the Greek writings of the New
Testament, which in some respects served to obscure for centuries
the Jewish matrix of Christianity.

The question of Christianity's remaining a Jewish sect inevitably
arose with the coming of converts from the pagan world. Jewish
converts to Christianity as a Jewish sect constituted no problem.
However, the decision of the Council of Jerusalem in A.D. 49, which

established the legitimacy of Gentile Christianity, represented a serious threat to the survival of Rabbinic Judaism since it raised serious question about the validity of the Law for Gentiles. Basic Jewish rites and ritual requirements were abrogated for Gentile Christian converts, and later, according to Paul, even for Jewish Christians. Although it should be noted that it was some time afterwards before it was decided that Jewish Christians were not bound to the Law of Judaism, for the Gentile, at least, the umbilical cord between Judaism and Christianity was cut; and a rift between the two faiths was inevitable. In freely opening its doors to the Gentile or pagan world, without entry to Christianity through Judaism, Judeo-Christianity was destined to be eclipsed by the missionary expansion of Hellenistic Christianity. The repudiation of any obligation to follow basic rules and ritual requirements of Judaism meant that Christianity's emergence as a separate movement was assured.

The early schism which arose between Judeo-Christians (Judaizers) and pagano-Christians (Gentiles) resulted in an antipathy between Judeo-Christianity and Hellenistic Christianity. Rabbinic Judaism manifested a growing hostility toward Hellenistic Christianity during the first century, primarily over the threat posed by the abrogation of the Law but also probably because by the end of the first century Christianity was a rival of Judaism for the conversion of the pagan world and Judaism did not want to incur any additional political disfavor from its identification with Christianity. The stoning of Stephen by Jews (Acts 7:54-60) and Paul's account of his own sufferings from Jews attest to the intensity of this growing conflict between Judaism and Christianity: "Five times," Paul wrote, "I was given the thirty-nine lashes by the Jews; . . . and once I was stoned" (II Cor. 11:16-29). In Asia Minor Paul and Barnabas were persecuted by Jews on their first and second missionary journeys (Acts 13:50-14:6; 17:5-18:17). In Lystra some Jews led a mob in stoning Paul and dragging him out of the city (Acts 14:19). At Corinth some Jews brought Paul and Barnabas before Gallio, the Roman governor of Greece (Acts 18:12-16). Finally, Paul is made a prisoner and taken to Rome upon the demand of Jews (Acts 28:17-22). In Paul's dramatic encounter with fellow-Jews in Rome, they inform Paul, "We would like to hear your ideas, for we do know that everywhere people speak against this party that you belong to." As has been

acknowledged by various scholars, the Talmud also reflects a
Jewish hostility toward first-century Christianity. References to
Jesus, while few in number, show a negative bias throughout.
According to the Talmud, Jesus was the illegitimate son of a soldier
named Panthera. In Egypt Jesus learned forms of magic which were
the basis of the miracles He performed. Jesus was legally executed
and His body was stolen by His disciples, who invented the story
of His resurrection. Finally, Jesus' teachings were evil and He
was a "deceiver of Israel." No less complimentary are the references
in the Talmud to Judeo-Christians, who are identified as "traitors" or
"betrayers." According to tradition, and not without some sub-
stantiation, Jews were responsible for persecutions and martyrdoms
of numerous Christians during the first century. By the end of that
century there was a move by Rabbinic Judaism to expel Christians
from the synagogue, a practice known as *asynagogos*. To Rabbinic
Judaism, to emphasize again, acceptance of the Christian Christ was a
Jewish impossibility, and the theological foundations of Judaism and
Christianity were irreconcilable. By the end of the first century, at
the Council of Jamnia in A.D. 90, Judaism had pronounced a curse
on Christianity as an apostasy. To both Palestinian and Diaspora
Jews, Christianity was a disavowal of Israel's God and Israel's Law.

Likewise, during the first century, Hellenistic Christianity increasingly manifested an antipathy toward both the Jews and the
Judaizers, the Judeo-Christians. Christianity, which clearly began as a
Jewish sect, gradually extricated itself from Judaism and became a
Gentile movement, quite distinctive and separated from Judaism. As
centuries later with the schismatic development of Protestantism out
of Catholicism, so Christianity emerged out of Judaism with a bias
against the Judaism of that period which Hellenistic Christianity
finally exhibited even toward Judeo-Christianity. In a profound
sense, while Christianity was the outgrowth of Judaism, usually
referred to by Christians as "the fulfillment of Judaism," Christianity
in reality became a new faith. Radically different from Judaism in
certain fundamental aspects of its theological character, Hellenistic
Christianity proclaimed its own interpretation of the faith of Israel as
viewed in the Jewish Scriptures, which Hellenistic Christianity
viewed as preparation for Christianity and the Christian Gospel. With
the destruction of the Temple in A.D. 70, the Hellenistic Christian
community was convinced that "the promises made to Israel" and

the prophecies of Jewish Scriptures had passed from the Jews to the Christians, and henceforth belong exclusively to the church, the new Israel, which, to Rabbinic Judaism, was a categorical denial of Israel's national character and mission.

The developing conflict between Judaism and Christianity finally reached its climax of hostility in a Christian theological explanation of the crucifixion which declared that "the Jews killed Jesus." The charge is one of the great ironies of history. The Jews are charged by Christianity, which began as a Jewish sect, with a crucifixion which was carried out by Romans against Jesus, a Jew, for a political crime. Ironically, and tragically, responsibility for the death of Jesus is, according to early Christian tradition, placed upon *the* Jews and not upon Pilate and certain Roman soldiers. According to Matthew 27:27, this Jewish guilt was acknowledged by the chief priests and the elders in their reported declaration, "His blood be on us and our children." The destruction of the Temple and the dispersion of the Jews which followed were interpreted by the early church as confirmation of the Jews' retribution for killing and rejecting Jesus, a *principle* of interpretation, it should be noted, which was not without some Jewish theological foundations, since it identified historical disasters visited upon Israel as the result of the peoples' sins. By contrast the Roman historian Tacitus, who of course was not a Christian, in A.D. 112 simply wrote that Jesus "was put to death as a criminal by Pontius Pilate." By the latter part of the second century Christian theologians, such as Justin Martyr in his *Dialogue with Trypho,* were writing that Jesus was crucified *under* Pontius Pilate but *by* the Jews. To add still further to the irony of the theological explanation of the crucifixion that the Jews killed Jesus, there developed the tradition in the church, as attested by Tertullian and Origen, that Pilate became a Christian. There are also references to Pilate as a saint, and he is so regarded by the Ethiopian Church to this day. Some apocryphal writings of the second century, such as the *Gospel of Peter,* completely exonerate Pilate of all guilt and place the blame for the crucifixion squarely on the Jews. This ancient theological judgment on the Jews became a major factor in the tragedy of Jewish-Christian relations in the centuries which followed, especially during the Middle Ages. As even recent studies have shown, such as Bernhard E. Olson's *Faith and Prejudice,* there is still a definite relationship between prejudice against the Jews and the theological charge that the Jews killed Jesus.

By the latter part of the second century Christian antipathy toward Judaism was even more clearly marked. Even Judeo-Christianity came to be regarded as heretical and Judeo-Christians were censured under the names of Ebionites, Quartodecimans, Encratites, Millenarianists, or, more especially, Judaizers. The writings of early Church Fathers, such as Justin Martyr and Ignatius, were now directed not only against Jews, but also against those Jewish Christians who were viewed as Judaizers. Parkes has written of the Judeo-Christians, "There is no more tragic group in Christian history than these unhappy people. They, who might have been the bridge between the Jewish and Gentile world, must have suffered intensely at the developments on both sides [Rabbinic Judaism and Hellenistic Christianity] which they were powerless to arrest. Rejected, first by the Church, in spite of their genuine belief in Jesus as the Messiah, and then by the Jews in spite of their loyalty to the Law, they ceased to be a factor of any importance in the development of either Christianity or Judaism."

From its transformation originally as a Jewish sect to a separate religion, Christianity by the fourth century was completely disengaged from Judaism and in conflict with both Judaism and Judeo-Christianity. Hellenistic Christianity's evaluation of Judaism and the Law came to be locked into Christian theology, aided by considerable reinforcement from the Church Fathers and later Christian theologians. In the centuries which followed, however, the complete break of Christianity with Judaism, no matter how regrettably it must be viewed, as surely it must, did in some ways symbolize the transmission of Christianity to the Gentile world and presage the universal role of Christianity as a missionary religion to the world. Christianity, no longer tied to any particular culture, race, or tradition, proclaimed that God is the God of the Gentiles as well as Jews (Rom. 3:29) and in Christ there is no longer any difference between Jews and Gentiles (Gal. 3:28). This universalism, however, must not obscure the fact that Christianity, which began as a Jewish sect, by the second century clearly reflected an anti-Jewish bias which today can only be lamented. By the second century the term Jew came to be used in a pejorative sense by Christian writers to refer to Jews as unbelievers, who, as Jews, were viewed as opponents of Christ and the Christian faith. So far as early Christian tradition was concerned, the Jews had been "abandoned by God," and the final "departure of the sceptre from Israel" had taken place with the advent of Christianity.

III

As painful as it may be for the Christian in the twentieth century to acknowledge, there can be no turning away from the historical reality that an anti-Jewish bias pervaded the writings of the Church Fathers, and that these writings largely fixed the tradition of Christian anti-Semitism which has permeated so much of Christian history. The tragedy of Christianity's anti-Jewish bias, reflected in centuries of malevolence and misdeeds against the Jews, has recently been referred to by one historian of religion, and with considerable justification, as "the crime of Christendom." The pejorative manner in which Jews and Judaism were referred to in the writings of early Christianity is clearly explicit from even a casual examination of the writings themselves.

The conflict which developed so early between Judaism and Christianity during the first century became even more intense during the second century. Christian writings reflected an increasingly anti-Jewish spirit, while Judaism became more antagonistic toward Christianity. That which constituted the very basis of the Christian faith, "Jesus Christ is Lord," was that which drove Judaism and Christianity farther and farther apart, since their respective claims, Torah and Christ, were mutually contradictory. The real tragedy of the theological conflict, however, lay in the nature of the conflict itself and the intense bitterness it evoked from Christians and from Jews. Each charged the other not just with religious or theological error, but with moral depravity and religious apostasy. What is more, both Judaism and Christianity lost sight of the profound truths and the theological heritage they both shared in common. The missionary expansion of Christianity throughout the Roman Empire stiffened the resistance of Judaism to Christianity, and this recalcitrant opposition of Jewish communities to conversion to Christianity in turn exasperated Christian communities which saw such resistance as an open defiance of God's purpose.

In Jewish-Christian dialogue today, Christians can ill afford to ignore the continuing conflict between Christianity and Judaism through the centuries. Bitter conflict characterized the entire patristic period of Christian history and this fact alone profoundly influenced the future course of Christian theology and Jewish-Christian relations. As a matter of fact, hostility toward the Jews and Judaism abound throughout patristic literature, in such writings as the *Epistle of Barnabas*, Justin Martyr's *Dialogue with Trypho*, Hippolytus' *Expository Treatise Against the Jews*, and the *Treatises of Cyprian*. Among the repeated charges against the Jews in these writings were that the Jews completely misunderstood the Law and misinterpreted the Scriptures, that Christ abrogated the Law, and that Jews, as killers of Jesus, were rejected by God and no longer His chosen people. So great was the estrangement that even the historical continuity of Christianity with Judaism was denied by early Church Fathers. Ignatius wrote, "Christianity did not base its faith on Judaism, but Judaism on Christianity." Early Church Fathers denied that the Old Testament had anything whatsoever to do with the Jews; rather, they maintained that the Old Testament had to do with the past of the church and not with the ancestors of contemporary Jews. Christianity early laid claim to a superior understanding of the Hebrew Scriptures than the Jews themselves possessed. Had not the Book of Hebrews been written to show the superiority of Christianity over the religion of Moses? The Church Fathers, as ecclesiastics and theologians throughout the Middle Ages, in their anti-Jewish polemics repeatedly charged the Jews with the death of Jesus, invariably offering the explanation for Jewish suffering as divine retribution for their sins. "Because of the crime of the Jews," Origen wrote, "the city [Jerusalem] perished utterly and the Jewish nation was overthrown." Augustine, a major architect of Catholic theology reaffirmed the same judgment: "But the Jews who rejected him and slew him after that were miserably ruined by the Romans and were dispersed over the face of the whole earth." Eusebius wrote that one of the purposes for writing his *Ecclesiastical History* was "to relate the misfortunes which have come upon the entire Jewish people as a result of their plots against our Saviour." Perhaps the most vitriolic attacks on Jews from a Christian source came from the "silver tongued" Chrysostom, the most famous preacher of the early church, who in 387 preached a series of eight anti-Jewish sermons at Antioch. Having charged the Jews with "deicide," a word he coined, he proclaimed, "I hate the Jews because they violate the Law. I hate the Synagogue because it has the Law and the Prophets. It is the duty of all Christians to hate the Jews." Centuries later Martin Luther echoed similar sentiments by writing that the destruction of the temple and subsequent dispersion of the Jews indicated "divine wrath" on the Jews and "show all too clearly that they are surely in error and on the wrong path." Examples of such denigration of the Jews, common even in twentieth-century Christian writings, Catholic and Protestant, have by no means been eradicated from contemporary Christianity, as recent studies have clearly shown.

Second only to its relations with a hostile state, the question of Jewish-Christian relations was the major problem which the early church faced for several centuries. Regrettably, many centuries passed before either the question of church-state relations or Jewish-Christian relations was resolved with any degree of adequacy. Actually, the two questions were historically and intimately interrelated. With Constantine's espousal of Christianity in the Edict of Milan of 313, the status of both Christianity and Judaism was dramatically and radically changed. On the one hand, Christianity, transformed from a persecuted faith to a tolerated one, was by 346 the persecutor of rival faiths within the Roman Empire. On the other hand, Judaism became a proscribed faith, its members increasingly subjected to alienation, discrimination, and humiliation by both the church and the state. The church allied with the state meant that the political power of the state was now available to implement the theological judgment which had so frequently been pronounced on the Jews in patristic writings. As Father Edward H. Flannery stated it in his painstaking account of Christian guilt for the persecution of the Jews, the political power of the church permitted "the translation into statutory form of what the patristic teaching seemed to call for." Thus repressive measures often accompanied by stringent regulations were enacted, such as proscribing any Jew upon threat of the death penalty from making a convert (which was to mark the termination of Jewish missionary efforts) and any Christian from participating in Jewish rites. Various Christian emperors sought to prohibit special religious observances, to regulate synagogue services, and even to compel Jews' converting to Christianity. The growing intolerance of the Christian world, along with a growing anarchy in the Roman Empire, resulted in a shift of the center of Jewry from the Roman Empire to Babylonia, where several million

Jews lived in relative freedom under an Exilarch until the tenth century. By the eleventh century increased Islamic restrictions on the Jews caused a shift of Judaism westward to Europe which remained the population center of Judaism for almost a thousand years.

The concept of the Christian state, which found classic expression in the *corpus Christianum,* provided a firm basis for the establishment of the Holy Roman Empire by Charlemagne in 800. This development in turn had a profound effect on Jewish-Christian relations in Europe. To be a citizen of the Empire was to be a member of the church, and to be a member of the church was the foundation of one's citizenship in the Empire. Enemies of the church were regarded as enemies of the state. Jews, since they obviously were not Christians, were therefore aliens without any citizenship and were thereby reduced to a pariah people, without real human status or civil rights. From the First Crusade in 1096, the Crusades marked the beginning of a new wave of vigorous persecutions, including massacres of entire Jewish communities. As religious aliens in a Christian state, Jews were subjected to repeated pogroms and expulsions—from England in 1290, from France in 1306, from Spain in 1492, and from German and Austrian cities during the fourteenth and fifteenth centuries. After the Middle Ages, the violent anti-Semitism of Martin Luther and the Counter Reformation, both aggravated by the refusal of Jews to become Christians in a Christian state, served to stimulate new waves of the Christian anti-Semitism which had so long plagued Christian history. Suffice it to say, for centuries prior to the French Revolution, non-toleration of Jews was a familiar and integral part of the basic religious policy of the leading nations of Europe. The emergence of political democracy, particularly the secular state, made possible the legal equality of different religious faiths, which was further reinforced after the latter part of the eighteenth century by the separation of church and state and legal guarantees of religious liberty.

It is not the purpose here to recount even in summary fashion the centuries of persecution and revilement accorded the Jews in Christendom, but these passing references have been made to suggest that the anti-Jewish bias which appeared early in Christianity has, to the shame of Christian history and Christian theology, been perpetuated by the church with recurring regularity through the centuries. What is more, this historic anti-Jewish bias has a manifest continuity with modern anti-Semitism which reached its terrifying climax in the Holocaust of Nazi Germany in which six million Jews were killed in the heart of what is historically termed "Christian Europe." Second only to the tragedy itself has been the deplorable fact that Christian anti-Semitism and Christian maltreatment of the Jews have been conspicuously missing from most Christian accounts of the history of Christianity. Surely this is not the time for an attitude of euphoria toward Jewish-Christian dialogue in the modern world, but it is certainly not the time for Christian inertia or silence either. Too much has happened in the past, including the all too recent past—the Holocaust, the creation of the State of Israel, the Six-Day War—to allow for moral apathy or any kind of escape from Christian responsibility in Jewish-Christian relations. There is, however, a profound need for an informed awareness of Jewish-Christian relations in some historical perspective, including a need for intellectual honesty in Christian historiography, but there is also the desperate need for a spirit of confession, penitence, and restitution for the Christian-Jewish tragedy of almost two thousand years. In a profound sense, the history of Jewish-Christian relations must be called a two-fold tragedy: a Jewish tragedy marked by Christian theological denigration and falsification of Judaism, accompanied by Jewish martyrology, and a Christian tragedy in its manifest contradiction of the ethical truths of Christian faith and in its repudiation of Christianity's Jewish theological heritage.

James E. Wood, Jr.

PART ONE

CONTEMPORARY JEWISH-CHRISTIAN RELATIONS

IN HISTORICAL PERSPECTIVE

Kirchenkampf and Holocaust:
The German Church Struggle and
Nazi Anti-Semitism in Retrospect

Franklin H. Littell

Jews have been writing their chronicles and histories—for Jews. Some Christian Scholars have been writing about the Church Struggle—for Christians. The deeper meaning of the Holocaust and *Kirchenkampf* has scarcely penetrated the American scene at all. Jewish leaders maintain that the American Jewish community has not yet come to terms with the Holocaust—for reasons which are certainly easy enough even for an outgrouper to understand. Less understandable, however, especially in view of the rising power of the Radical Right in America, is the failure of the American churches to work through the lessons of the German church struggle. Even the theological schools give it only a passing glance, chiefly because it does not fit the kind of self-understanding which American Christendom has of itself. Thirty years ago, as the Confessing Church was going to its Synod at Bad Oeynhausen or the German Jews were facing the dreadful portent of the *Kristalnacht,* there were only two leading churchmen in America who repeatedly and clearly—and with interpretations which still stand the test of time—warned of the true import of Nazism's war against the Jews *and* the Christians: Reinhold Niebuhr and George Shuster. Today, so far as the churches are concerned, it is only among the students and younger theologians that the questions which the *Kirchenkampf* and the Holocaust put to traditional religious institutions constantly arise.

It is therefore with great anticipation and gratitude that the Wayne State University's undertaking to develop a major documentation and research center on the Church Struggle and a North American center on the Holocaust is to be welcomed by a whole company of

---

This article was originally delivered 16 March 1970 as an address at the International Scholars Conference on the German Church Struggle: 1933-1945, sponsored by Wayne State University.

scholars. The Wayne Project signalizes, among other things, the way energetic concern for religion as an intellectual discipline is moving out of the church ghettos into the state universities. It also gives promise that the most important events of recent generations of religious history may at last get the general attention they deserve. It is not too much to say that the vigorous intellectual and practical work of the Dutch churches, both Catholic and Protestant, and of a substantial sector of the churches in Germany, is a result in good part of their mastery of the lessons of the Church Struggle and the Holocaust. And the confusion on the American religious scene, in spite of fleeting references to ecumenism, church renewal, and interfaith dialogue from time to time, seems to document that we are still working very largely with the concepts and assumptions of nineteenth century culture-religion, of the happy time before the flood waters covered the earth.

Most encouraging is the extent to which various aspects of the problematic have caught the attention and inspired the hard work of scholars outside the theological field: historians, political scientists, sociologists, social psychologists, educators, and psychologists. Since a totalitarian system by definition seeks to conquer all aspects of life from architecture to zoology, such a broad sweep of academic concern is appropriate.[1] It also signifies another very important theoretical consideration: that the major theological problems may often be illuminated not by professionals, who dig like moles ever deeper into the old and proven veins of sustenance, but by so-called "laymen" working in so-called "secular" disciplines and idioms.

I. THE THEOLOGICAL MEANING OF NATIONAL SOCIALISM

In theological terms, Nazism was the true—if illegitimate—offspring of a false relationship between the Christian church and the ethnic bloc or nation *(volk)*. And it has its analogues today in places as distant from each other as Alabama and South Africa, Belfast and Beirut. When ethnic history is infused with "spirituality," and a political program is mounted on disciplined cadres to return a people to a mythical monism of the past, a frontal challenge to the true church—on pilgrimage and supra-national—is thrown down. The

---

1. Franklin H. Littell, *Wild Tongues: A Handbook of Social Pathology* (New York: Macmillan Co., 1969), p. 93.

situation is confused, however, because most of the baptized will accommodate (e.g., in *Kirchenausschüsse)* or apostatize (e.g., in White Citizens' Councils) rather than give the head of the church the undivided loyalty they once promised Him.

It was the glory of the Confessing Church to have perceived that a frontal confrontation was involved, and no mere issue of everyday politics in a disaster area. The fact that some saw the sweeping dimensions of the struggle sooner than others, and that even the *Bekennende Kirche* did not immediately understand the meaning of hatred of the Jews as hatred of the Jew, Jesus of Nazareth, does not detract one iota from the debt the whole church owes the men of Barmen and what they did. Karl Barth put it directly: "National Socialism, according to its own revelation of what it is—a self-revelation to which it has devoted all the time and chance till now allowed—is as well without any doubt something quite different from a political experiment. It is, namely, a *religious institution of salvation.*" Again, "It is impossible to understand National Socialism unless we see it in fact as a *new Islam.*"[2] And the men who presented the Memorandum of May 1936 to the *Führer* of the Third Reich rightly identified the offense to the true church: "When blood, race, nationality, and honour are regarded as eternal values the first commandment obliges the Christian to refuse this evaluation. When the Aryan is glorified, the Word of God teaches that all men are sinful. If the Christian is faced by the Anti-Semitism of the Nazi *Weltanschauung* to hate the Jews, he is, on the contrary, bidden by the Christian Commandment to love his neighbor."[3] Dietrich Bonhoeffer, martyred as the war was ending, drew one concrete conclusion—but a conclusion on which there is still little guidance in Christian theological literature: "If we claim to be Christians there is no room for expediency. Hitler is the Anti-Christ. Therefore we must go on with our work and eliminate him whether he is successful or not."[4]

The problem of discerning and defining the Christian obligation

---

2. Karl Barth, *The Church and the Political Problem of Our Day* (New York: Charles Scribner's Sons, 1939), pp. 41,43.
3. Hugh Martin et al., *Christian Counter-Attack* (New York: Charles Scribner's Sons, 1944), p. 135.
4. Dietrich Bonhoeffer, *Gesammelte Schriften,* ed. Eberhard Bethge (Munich: Kaiser Verlag, 1958), 1:297-298.

and style of resistance to illegitimate authority, not to mention illegitimate action by legitimate authority, remains one of the most excruciating agonies of Christians today. The word "anti-Christ" is the clue; for the anti-Christ is not the honest and open adversary, but the one who was once numbered within and has now gone over to the opposition. The misery of the Church Struggle is not in the first place battle with an open opposition; it is the apostasy of the baptized, the convulsion of Christendom.

Before the Church Struggle with Nazism, the Christian corpus gave very little guidance on the matter of resistance.[5] Representative government, in which each citizen shares the responsibility (and on occasion the guilt) for policies implemented by heads of state, is too new a thing in human history for any large body of interpretation to have emerged. But the experiences of the Third Reich remind us that not only must absolute monarchs who rule by divine right be warned and confronted on occasion, but also those governments which claim to have substantial—if sometimes "silent"—majorities acquiescing in their actions. In a police state, without free access or egress, the moral burden of national wrong-doing is certainly no greater than in a society which still has some room for organizing public opinion and pressure.

Even in the strictest Marxist areas, however, the lessons of the Church Struggle are bearing fruit. The influence of Bonhoeffer is marked. Western leaders have sometimes criticized Christians in East Germany because they did not denounce Marxism too as a "new Islam" and declare unqualified resistance. In this struggle, however, the first concern has been for the integrity and authenticity of the church—not to defend an ideological Christendom. What is at stake is not Christendom vs. a Marxist state-church, but the freedom of a true church to serve the human person. To this end, the state must be secularized, not re-Christianized—i.e., rendered modest, problem-solving, theologically speaking "creaturely." In this respect, the existence-problem of Christians in a Marxist state is not strikingly different from their problem in a society retrogressively committed to "Christendom," nor is it different from that of Christians living under sacral governments in the Arab League.

---

5. Bernhard Pfister and Gerhard Hildmann, eds., *Widerstandsrecht und Grenzen der Staatsgewalt* (Berlin: Duncker & Humblot, 1956).

II. SECULARIZATION VS. "SPIRITUALITY"

It is quite wrong to assume that the Church Struggle was a battle to defend Christian Germany against the false teaching of neo-barbarians, just as it is wrong to assume that the tragedy of this age is the arrival of a second great age of the persecutions. The tragedy is the wholesale apostasy of the baptized—their eagerness, in the name of "saving the world from atheistic Communism" and "reestablishing law and order" (and let us not forget that Hitler came to popular support and power on these two slogans), to countenance the most brutal and un-Christian of political measures to reconstitute a lost age of religious monism. "Apostasy," not "persecution," is the key word. And precisely for this reason the question which comes to us out of the Church Struggle concerns the nature of the church, the measure of human liberty, the future of the human person.

If we go forward into liberty, we must accept pluralism, voluntaryism, and dialogue as the qualities of religious maturity. Consonant to that is acceptance of the secularization process in significant sectors of society: government, social welfare, public education, higher education, the family.[6] Believing Jews and Christians must learn to distinguish "religion-in-general" *(positives Christentum,* to use the Nazi phrase) and a formless "spirituality" *(Geistigkeit),* and here any critical mind can join them, from a faith commitment authenticated by life in history—earthy, concrete. As Hans Buchheim put it in a fine study, "The claim of the National Socialists that there has never been for a long time so much 'believing' as in some sense in the year 1933 or the time of the war, is not false; yet it was in every respect an emptied faith, a faith false in content, intention and style."[7] For the Christian, at least, the anchor by which a vague "faith" or "love of humanity" or "spirituality" can be prevented from floating into the maelstrom of demonic ethnic religion (Teutonic, Arab, Anglo-Saxon, African, or pan-Slav) is precisely his identification with the Israel of God. For him the final version is not *Volksgemeinschaft* but the Kingdom of God, in which the peoples and tribes of the farthest corners of the earth shall gather

---

6. Franklin H. Littell, "The Secular City and Christian Self-Restraint," chap. 6 in *The Church and the Body Politic* (New York: Seabury Press, 1969).
7. Hans Buchheim, *Glaubenskrise im Dritten Reich* (Stuttgart: Deutsche Verlags-Anstalt, 1953), p. 17.

about the Hill of the Lord and hear His voice and do His will.

The Gentiles, however, can apostatize; they can take on the protective coloration of their pre-baptismal identity and disappear back into the tribe and pre-history. And when they do, they leave exposed *the Jew*, the one who—whether he is personally a believer or not—is a sign to the God of Abraham, Isaac, and Jacob. In a way which is mysterious and awesome, the Jews who perished in Hitler's Europe perished for a truth which the Christians—except for those who stayed Christian and were also hated and persecuted—betrayed: that the Author and Judge of history was made manifest to us out of the Jews. The tragic truth, which the Christian culture-religionists have not begun to grasp, is the truth that most of the martyrs for Christ in the twentieth century were Jews.

The moral claims of "religion-in-general" died at Auschwitz and Theresienstadt. The pretensions of the Christian intellectuals to a love for humanity—quite divorced from love, even compassion, toward specific persons and groups—foundered on the mechanical precision of the Nazi extermination of European Jewry. The German intellectual, overcome by a kind of spiritual vertigo as he contemplated the vast stretch of humanity, settled for national "we-feeling," for ethnic (Teutonic) identity which automatically excluded the Jews. And, as Koppel Pinson showed in a fine study thirty-five years ago,[8] the prevailing combination of Protestant Liberalism and Pietism prepared him for that submission to a false particularity. The true particularity, which points at the end to a true humanism, is the truth stated by Pope Pius XI, "We are spiritual Semites," and by Krister Stendahl, "Christians are a special kind of Jews." In a mysterious way, the very particularity of the Jews is the specific against a genocidal folk-identity which follows on regression into ethnicity infused with piety. In this stage of history, the particularity of the Jews is a testimony to universalism; it is the scandal on which all Gentile racism breaks its teeth. The frenetic effort artificially to reconstitute a religious monolith after the gods have died—whether that monolith be the *deutsche Glaube*, or "Christian America," or Islam—invariably leads from a latent hatred of the Jews to the overt forms of attack.

---

8. Koppel S. Pinson, *Pietism in the Rise of German Nationalism* (New York: Columbia University Press, 1936), passim.

For those who will join me in repudiation of "religion-in-general" and "spirituality" without content or integrity, but who are not prepared to accept the Christian theological formulation, let me state it this way: we are so situated, in our various national and racial contexts, that we cannot in fact love humanity without loving concrete, earthy, historic persons and groups. Under pressure, we shall either retrogress to a first love of the Gentile tribe or nation, or we shall love that Israel whose prophets and seers point us toward a day of universal justice and righteousness, mercy, and peace. Hatred of the Jews is often the first seismographic reading of the covert emergence of a false particularism, and we must learn to recognize it as such.

Precisely for this reason we should bring together as at the International Conference at Wayne State University, *Kirchenkampf* and Holocaust. For Christians—and not just for the Jewish people—the Holocaust is the most important event in recent church history. For working theologians, it has called into question the whole fabric of Christendom, indeed the very language of traditional religion, just as among youth and students it has rendered the churches incredible. For scholars of other disciplines and vernaculars, political anti-Semitism is a code to identify the totalitarian ideologies and systems which are the curse of the twentieth century—whether our eyes are turned toward "the Jews of silence" of Soviet Russia, the Jews of the State of Israel (which Nasser promised in a public address on 26 May 1967 to exterminate), or the Jews, our fellow citizens, who are the special target of the Radical Right.

Reference was made to the false "spirituality" which was so strong in the Third Reich, and against which the men of Barmen and the Confessing Church made their particular stand. In practical terms, the interchangeability of this base core of devotion was recognized by Hitler himself. He told Rauschning on one occasion: "There is more that binds us to Bolshevism than separates us from it. . . . I have always made allowance for this circumstance and have given orders that former Communists be admitted to the Party at once."[9] For a "true believer" of totalitarian type, one closed system may be viewed as good as another!

---

9. Quoted in Horace M. Kannen, *Secularism Is the Will of God* (New York: Twayne Publishers, 1954), p. 162n.

III. The Treason of the Intellectuals

In theological terms, it is this interchangeability which gives
special pathos to the irresponsibility of the German intellectuals. For
while the common folk were left to the credulity and quick switch of
the "true believer," the liberal academies had been very largely
rendered incapable of *any* unqualified loyalties—especially to institutional religion! Yet in the end they proved as unable to stand against
the claims of the *Volksgemeinschaft* as the most unlettered farmer or
laborer. Looking on from the balcony, the men of universities and
professions were quite able to perceive the naive and faulty character
of unquestioned obedience to any party or group. But again, when
the day of reckoning came they were without moorings to withstand
the overpowering demands of the ideological one-party state. As
Albert Einstein noted in a famous statement, resistance came not
from the universities but primarily from simple Christian laymen and
their pastors. The people of the congregations who remained faithful,
and the pastors who held true to the covenant, were living at a level
of trust which men who lived from the Fall, from *Techne*, could
neither identify with nor understand.

A "spirituality" which has no relation to a known tradition, a
"religious moment" which involves no loyalties to a known
alternative, is what contemporary political gnosticism offers us. But
the gnosticism—the closed system of secret knowledge—of the
twentieth century carries political force not noted in the Gnostic
heresies which tormented the early church.[10] "Faith" which is
divorced from Judaism or Christianity, the "faith in faith" of which
Will Herberg wrote in his classic review of the American Religion,
Protestant/Catholic/Jew,[11] in our day sooner or later finds a
political channel.

Then let our view of the future (and it is precisely the hope of
things to come which gives history its meaning and shape) be
governed by a clear vision. As Jüngen Moltmann has written in his
Theology of Hope in criticism of the vague perspectives which mar
the contemporary neo-Liberalism, the transposed eschatology of the
Greek *moment*, the *Nun* of existentialism, is far different from the

---

10. Eric Voegelin, *The New Science of Politics* (Chicago: University of Chicago Press,
1952), passim.
11. Will Herberg, *Protestant, Catholic, Jew* (Garden City, N.Y.: Doubleday, 1955).

promise given Israel: "It is one thing to ask: where and when does an epiphany of the divine, eternal, immutable and primordial take place in the realm of the human, temporal and transient? And it is another thing to ask: when and where does the God of the promise reveal his faithfulness and in it himself and his presence?"[12] We are thrust back upon the essential Jewishness of our *Heilsgeschichte*—in spite of all awareness of the dangers of a linear view of history, pointed out by contextual ethicists and illuminated by linguistic analysis. The truth is that we shall as a people either look for an epiphany in the American religion, which George Wallace has a better chance to declare than Harvey Cox, or Peter Berger, or Martin Marty, or we shall confess—however haltingly—the vision of Isaiah for the time to come. The irony of our recent decades is severe: those who have found the particularity of "Jewish folklore and fable" too confining, too earthy, too finite, have ended in the pitiful vulgarisms of Teutonic or Anglo-Saxon or other Gentile ethnicity.

Gandhi was once asked to state his greatest grief, and he answered, "the hardness of heart of the educated." It may be that Søren Kierkegaard's iconoclastic word can fix the point: ". . . the greater a man's equipment of knowledge and culture, the more difficult it is for him to become a Christian."[13] This means, for the purposes of this discussion, it is harder for him to accept involvement, commitment. Romain Rolland telegraphed an international congress of philosophers just before the opening of World War I: "Think as men of action. Act as men of thought." This has not been the record; in the face of one totalitarian threat after another, the men of the universities have copped out. Søren Kierkegaard's presentation of "the Professor" certainly remains the most perceptive exposure of that permanent tentativeness, that spectator's stance, wherein the confusion of the scientific objectivity of accurate reporting and the moral objective of the irresponsible has reduced technical progress to frivolity and self-destruction. You may recall "the Professor" who, if he could have seen the crucifixion would have asked, if possible, to have it repeated, that he could be sure to have an accurate report of all the details! My hope is that we shall not hesitate to draw some of

---

12. Jürgen Moltmann, *Theology of Hope,* trans. James W. Leitch (New York: Harper & Row, 1967), p. 43.
13. Quoted in Gabriel Vahanian, *The Death of God* (New York: George Braziller, 1961), p. 225.

the necessary, if painful, conclusions to be drawn by study of the
Church Struggle and the Holocaust—even when those conclusions
come close to home, even when the lessons cast long shadows across
the present state of religion and politics in the United States!

Bonhoeffer, of course, knew the academic world well. And he
knew the terrible prejudice against involvement *(Engagement)* in
conflict, especially "political" conflict. Many of the opponents of
the *Gleichschaltung* of the universities, and of the *Dozentführer*
installed by the Party, took the conservative ground: the university,
as a reservation for objective scholarship and research, must be kept
free of turmoil and conflict. (We hear the same elitist arguments
now, from those who criticize in faculty meeting the involvement of
their faculty colleagues in anti-Vietnam protests and stop by the
office afterwards to pick up their checks for defense research.) The
conservatives of the German universities scorned the vulgarization of
the Nazi effect, and dishonored the classical standards which had
made the scholarship of German universities the center of the literate
world. What a difficult decision it was for Bonhoeffer, who knew and
loved this Academe—and could have survived the war in a theological
faculty in America (while carrying on scholarly work, of course)—to
decide to go back home. Morally, it meant to reaffirm involvement in
that most ambiguous of civil acts, tyrannicide. Professionally, it
meant to abandon forever any chance of enjoying the academic
preserve of "objectivity," of non-complicity. The decision to oppose
Nazism was long since made; the decision to cut off the world of
liberal scholarship and those who defend its aloofness with such
feline passion, was the last and hardest step.

In discussing the lessons of *Kirchenkampf* and Holocaust for the
man of the university we are not only speaking of university-trained
mechanics—technicians with university degrees who were as empty of
humane education as the bookkeeper at Dachau or the plumber at
Bergen-Belsen, and just as ready to follow orders. We are referring to
university men of humanistic training. Wherein was the treason of
the intellectuals?

If we turn to a specific element, to the professors and writers of
German liberal Protestantism, perhaps we shall learn something
about the peculiar perils of our vocation, and also gain a clue as to
why liberal Protestantism in America today is so endemically—if
usually covertly—anti-Semitic. For the truth is (and this is the
tragedy of the intellectuals in many places during the century) that

the academics have proven ineffectual in the face of totalitarian thrusts for power and shatteringly confused in the face of the most inhumane of all modern irrationalities: hatred of the Jews.

Looking back on the Church Struggle, in which he played such an important fraternal part, Josef L. Hromadka once wrote: "The liberal theology in Germany and in her orbit utterly failed. It was willing to compromise on the essential points of divine law and of 'the law of nature'; to dispose of the Old Testament and to accept the law of the Nordic race instead; and to replace the 'Jewish' law of the Old Testament by the autonomous law of each race and nation respectively. It had made all the necessary preparation for the 'Germanization of Christianity' and for a racial Church."[14] Nor is the problem yet resolved in German Protestantism, in spite of the testimony of the Confessing Church. As Samuel Sandmel pointed out in a critical essay on Rudolf Bultmann's treatment of Judaism, the danger point remains exposed. In contrast to the early church, where—except for Marcion—Jesus and His message were understood to be a continuation of Judaism, Professor Bultmann presses Judaism into the cramped mold of a distorted view of the Law; he describes "a Judaism that never existed so that he can set a special view of Jesus over against it."[15] The parallel to Arnold Toynbee's rejection of the Jews as a "Semitic fossil" is striking.[16] Both reveal the covert anti-Semitism of liberal culture-religion. And the references explain why they and their colleagues and followers instinctively respond in opposition to the current manifestations of religious renaissance in world Jewry.

The problem of liberal anti-Semitism is far more dangerous in America, however, for we have here the last major sector of Christendom which still lives relatively undisturbed in the balmy days of nineteenth century culture-religion. The lessons to be learned from *Kirchenkampf* and Holocaust have hardly penetrated our

---

14. Josef L. Hromadka, *Doom and Resurrection* (Richmond: Madrus House, 1945), p. 102; for more extensive discussion of this point, with citations, see my "The Protestant Churches and Totalitarianism (Germany 1933-1945)," in *Totalitarianism*, ed. Carl J. Friedrich (Cambridge, Mass.: Harvard University Press, 1954), pp. 108-119.

15. Samuel Sandmel, "Bultmann on Judaism," in *The Theology of Rudolf Bultmann*, ed. Charles W. Kegley (New York: Harper and Row, 1966), p. 218.

16. Arnold J. Toynbee, *A Study of History* (New York: Oxford University Press, 1957), pp. 8, 22; see the brilliant critique by D. Eric Voegelin in *Order and History*, vol. 1, *Israel and Revelation* (Baton Rouge: Louisiana State University Press, 1956), p. 120.

Protestant seminaries, our liberal Protestant press, our church literature, the thinking and writing of even our ablest older theologians.

For example, there was constituted some months ago, under the auspices of the National Council of Churches and the National Conference of Catholic Bishops, a working party of twenty prominent theologians to deal with the problematic: "Israel: the People, the Land, the State." First, in an effort to get behind everyday politics and humanitarian concerns, attention was fixed upon these theological issues: (1) "The Promised Land and Our Responsibilities"; (2) "Our Responsibility for the Holocaust—The Significance of Hatred of the Jews in the History of Christianity, The Significance of Hatred of the Jews in Islam, The Uniqueness of the Holocaust"; and (3) "Our Christian Responsibility for Reconciliation."[17] Letters were sent to heads of seminaries and graduate departments of religion, on the chance that somewhere Biblical and church historical studies might be going forward which would widen and deepen the discussion. Shortly thereafter a letter arrived from the dean of a seminary which considers itself the bulwark of American Liberal Protestantism. The relevant sentences are as follows:

After reading the topics I must say that I am dismayed and wish to register my strongest protest. If the Christian Church is really concerned for reconciliation in the world, not least in the Middle East, I can think of many more fruitful approaches than this kind of question begging and special pleading effort. The topics are so loaded as to be hardly more than one more propaganda effort to put American Christian support behind present Israeli policies. If peace and reconciliation in the Middle East is one of our fundamental concerns why set up programs that tie in the word like "responsibility" to what is a patently Zionist line of thought. The Christian response to anti-Semitism is surely not Semitism.[18]

Probably the last sentence is the most revealing. For the purpose of this argument the salient points are these: "objectivity" has led to a rejection of overt involvement in this earthy conflict and the debate which attends it; "humanity" has become the enemy of any avowed concrete attachments; and a general religious and ethical framework

17. Letter to seminary heads, dated 20 January 1970.
18. Correspondence in the writer's possession, dated 7 February 1970.

has led to rejection of any special holy history, especially any that had to do with the Jews. In consequence, when push comes to shove, the covert *Kulturantisemitismus* erupts into implied charges that behind the theological study of a group of troubled theologians must lie a sinister Zionist influence.

American Liberal Protestantism is sick, and the theological form of its sickness can be summarized by saying that it stands solidly on the ground but lately vacated by the *Deutsche Christen* (German Christians). The inevitable result of such academic aloofness and doctrinal uncertainty in the German universities and churches was the fatal weakening of the two centers which might have been the chief barriers to the Nazi system. More than that, they predictably produced a generation which came to power amiably inclined toward "spirituality" and "religion-in-general," but ill-informed as to the particular claims of the Christian faith.

Although there were in fact great differences of opinion among the Nazi leaders concerning the church, the result of the Party's emphasis was that an increasing number of members left the churches and registered themselves as "believers" without affiliation *(gottgläubig)*. The leaders who were not hostile appear to have been poorly informed as to Christian doctrine. Many displayed that emancipation toward historic community and confession of faith which Article 24 of the NSDAP Platform encouraged: "The party as such represents the point of view of a positive Christianity without binding itself to any particular confession. It fights the spirit of Jewish materialism. . . ." Goering's statement during the trial at Nürnberg seems to have been typical: "I myself am not what you might call a churchgoer, but I have gone now and then, and have always considered I belonged to the Church and have always had those functions over which the Church presides—marriage, chris-tening, burial, *et cetera*—carried out in my house by the Church."[19] This is about as clear a statement based on culture-religion as one is likely to find; it implies the privatization of religion, and, should conflict arise between state and church, leaves no doubt as to which of the two receives supreme loyalty.

The most complete formulation of a Christianity which

---

19. Herman Goering, *Trial of the Major War Criminals*, 42 vols. (Nürnberg: International Military Tribunal, 1947), 9:268.

accommodated doctrinally was made by the *Deutsche Christen,* and
the best written statement of that position would seem to be Cajus
Fabricius' *Positive Christianity in the Third Reich.* Basing his
rejection of any objective Semitic basis or unassimilatable dogmatic
formulae upon his nineteenth century liberal notion of experiential
and non-dogmatic religion, Fabricius set out to define the new
religion of Germany "in accordance with the basic principles of
National Socialism." He was sure that Christianity and National
Socialism had the same basic principles because they both have
"grown and become as one with the spirit of the German nation
throughout the history of centuries." "The living religion of the *Volk*
cannot be confined within a narrow scheme. . . ."[20] Such a "narrow
scheme" would be historical or doctrinal definition which challenged
the mystical base of the *Volksgemeinschaft*—an entity which Hitler
said would be the Nazis' "greatest contribution."

The men of the Christian resistance did not view holy history or
doctrine so light-heartedly, although they did not always speak as
bluntly as Hermann Sasse, who said, "The Evangelical Church has to
start every discussion with the avowal that its doctrine is a
permanent affront to the morality and ethical feeling of the German
race."[21] Nevertheless, they spoke plainly enough to be accused
constantly of "meddling in politics," to be charged with "fundamentalism" for asserting doctrines not negotiable, and to be
answered by a swarm of pamphlets like the neo-Lutheran "Ansbach
Counsel" (11 June 1943) which affirmed a general revelation made
manifest in the nation and its divinely appointed *Führer.*

One is inevitably reminded of the ecstatic affirmation of "non-
sectarian religion" to be found in Robert Welch's *The Blue Book:*

I believe there is a broader and more encompassing faith to which we can all
subscribe. . . . And I believe it is an ennobling conception, equally acceptable to
the most Fundamentalist Christian or the most rationalist idealist, because its
whole purpose is to strengthen and synthesize the ennobling characteristics of
each man and the ennobling impulses of his own personal religion.

It is hard for man to realize that the Infinite still remains infinite, untouched in

20. Cajus Fabricius, *Positive Christianity in the Third Reich* (Dresden: Püschel, 1937),
pp. 23-24.
21. J. Beckman, ed., *Kirchliches Jahrbuch, 1933-1944* (Gütersloh: C. Bertelsmann Verlag,
1948), p. 3.

Its remoteness and unreduced in Its infinity by man's most ambitious approaches or that all of man's increasing knowledge leaves the Unknowable just as completely unknowable as before. But I think that, being allowed now to grasp this truth, we should cease to quarrel and disagree over how close we are to God. For we are using a term which, in a literal context, or objectively, has no meaning.[22]

This is, from a Biblical point of view, the language of atheism. From the point of view of fascists, it avoids the reproach of outright atheism by appearing tolerant and *gottgläubig*.

The *Deutsche Christen* were at least logical enough to press the religion of the ethnic base, infused with "spirituality," through to its logical conclusion: anti-Semitism. In their 1932 Platform they appealed to all Christians "of German type" and affirmed "heroic piety." Repudiating all confessional parties, they cited the experience of German foreign missions which "have for a long time called to the German nation: 'Keep yourself racially pure.'" They then went on to condemn association with Jews, especially inter-marriage, and even missions to the Jews—"the entryway for foreign blood into our national body."[23]

IV. CONCLUSION

Now to return to the original question: the relationship of *Kirchenkampf* and Holocaust. When an effort is made to cut Christianity from its essentially Semitic base, when an artificial effort is made to reestablish the myth of Christendom, when the culture-religion of a Gentile race or nation becomes infused with spirituality and historic destiny, we are face to face with the Adversary. Those who attempted to domesticate the church, to make it in corrupted form a mere creature of the state, were of necessity compelled to do two things of grave theological import. For one thing, they were driven to oppose international contacts, to close off all communication with the *Ecumene*. The importance of the *Kirchenkampf* and the universal Christian fellowship to each other is

---

22. Robert Welch, *The Blue Book* (Boston: privately printed, 1959), pp. 68-69, 147.
23. Translated in full in Franklin H. Littell, *The German Phoenix* (New York: Doubleday, 1960), Appendix A.

an extensive theme, treated on another occasion.[24] Martin Bormann's model program for the "final solution to the church problem," subsequently published and ably analyzed in the German *Kommission's* volume on the Warthegau,[25] gives further evidence of how important Bormann—the ablest and most implacable of Christianity's enemies in the Nazi inner circle—thought cutting off contacts with the world Christian fellowship to be. On the second matter, the "final solution to the Jewish problem," the church—even the hard core of the Confessing Church—did less well; and the elimination of European Jewry is the one plank of Hitler's platform in which he could count a major success.

In the final paroxysms of "Christendom," as anxious powers strive to resist the process of secularization and the pattern of pluralism which modernity has thrust upon it, Jews and Christians of the pilgrim church have alike been sacrificed to bad politics and lowgrade Gentile religion. The crisis in credibility faced by the churches, which has alienated the youth and students and driven the younger theologians to seek a new form of words, has created a wasteland where only a few flowers of renewal give color and bring hope. One is reminded of a child's poem which survived the extermination center at Theresienstadt, where fifteen thousand Jewish children were murdered.

> Then,
> A week after the end,
> Everything will be empty here.
> A hungry dove will peck for bread.
> In the middle of the street will stand
> An empty, dirty
> Hearse.[26]

Even in America, behind the facade of statistical and institutional success are heard the rumblings of the preliminary stages of a church struggle which affects even the budgets of the boards and agencies. Pathological study of the German *Kirchenkampf* can teach us a great deal about the political and theological realities of the twentieth

---

24. "Die Bedeutung des Kirchenkampfes fur die Okumene," *Evangelische Theologie* 29 (1960): 1-21.
25. Paul Gürtler, *Nationalsozialismus und evangelische Kirchen im Warthegau* (Göttingen: Vandenhoeck & Ruprecht, 1958), Appendix Doc. 8, pt. 4.
26. Hana Volavkova, ed., *I Never Saw Another Butterfly . . . : Children's Drawings and Poems from Terczin Concentration Camp, 1942-1944* (New York: McGraw-Hill Book Co., 1962), p. 13.

century. One of these realities is the fact that retrogression to sacral society, to a mythical and therefore false harmony, is accompanied by outbursts against the historical Jewish people—even before "the struggle of the church against the church for the church" [27] sets in. The Jew, who cannot disappear into pre-history, is a surrogate for the Christian who can.

I have not sought to depreciate the witness of those academics or patriots who as men who loved culture or their country, or both, have fought anti-Semitism. I was profoundly moved to read Yevgeni Yevtushenko's poem "Babi Yar," to which Elie Wiesel called my attention in his book, *The Jews of Silence.* A Gentile, Yevtushenko has borne political and social opprobrium for a patriotism which is humane—a rare thing in any part of the world these days!

> Let the 'Internationale' ring out
> When the last anti-Semite on earth is buried.
> There is no Jewish blood in mine,
> But I am hated by every anti-Semite as a Jew,
> And for this reason,
> I am a true Russian.[28]

Anti-Semitism can no longer be handled as a humanitarian issue. The very term "anti-Semitism," which we use because it has become part of the language since the nineteenth century humanitarian pleas, is inaccurate and misleading—one of its most violent expressions is mounted in recent decades by "Semites," or Arabs, to whom the Holy War *(jihad)* against the Jews of Israel is a religious obligation. Islam, in dissolution, is producing many of the same frantic responses as Christendom in decay. Of these, the most blasphemous is hatred of the Jews.

For me, the problem is basically theological; it concerns the nature of man, his ultimate loyalty, his final identity, and his end-time *(eschaton).* The nature of the historical process is itself at stake as well as its consummation. Such affirmations cannot be proved inductively, since they are not objects of "the historical method," and so will not likely commend themselves immediately to all scholars. We can, however, establish in negative terms and critical analyses the indissoluble relationship of *Kirchenkampf* and

---

27. Arthur C. Cochrane, *The Church's Confession Under Hitler* (Philadelphia: Westminster Press, 1962), p. 19.
28. Elie Wiesel, *The Jews of Silence: A Personal Report on Soviet Jewry* (New York: Holt, Rinehart & Winston, 1966), p. 136.

Holocaust. As for the question whether Jews and Christians share a common future, which may move a theologian to read and think about the evidence, each of us must use his own vernacular; and if we achieve at least a partial pentecost we shall also begin to understand each other's languages in the university and to do something for interdisciplinary cooperation. As we do that, we shall again begin to speak for man—and not continue to contribute to his fragmentation, alienation, and dehumanization at the hands of political and academic machines. We shall also perceive that the most awful figure of this century is the technically competent barbarian—especially when he claims the sanction of religion for his politics of pride.

The Nemesis of Christian Antisemitism[1]

A. ROY ECKARDT

One could describe and celebrate Christian friendship and even love for Jews in past and present, but this would fill a wholly different assignment from the subject at hand. I speak as a committed Christian and churchman who is also concerned for objective historical scholarship.

The long history of evil treatment of the Jewish people at the hands of Christians means that a certain tension lurks beneath any meeting between Christians and Jews. Those who find psychological conflict unbearable may offer the following advice to speakers and leaders at such encounters: "Do not call attention to the guilt of the one side for what it has done to the other side. The guilty party will become self-defensive and the other party will be disconcerted. Both sides may very well take out their unhappiness on you." This advice is discarded in the presentation that follows. In genuine dialogue not only candor is needed, but, even more, there is need for truthfulness.

I

No concept is more relevant to the morphology and life of Christian antisemitism than "nemesis." "Nemesis" involves an act of retribution. Throughout Christian history the church has sought to justify its anti-Jewishness and anti-Judaism through association with

1. The present article is dedicated to Dr. James Parkes, the noted British historian, Anglican clergyman, and pioneering scholar in Jewish-Christian understanding. Parkes rightly identifies the spelling "anti-Semitism" as "pseudo-scientific mumbo jumbo" that implies that the phenomenon in question is somehow a movement directed against an actual quality called "Semitism." The word "antisemitism" is "not a scientific word, and it is entitled to neither a hyphen nor a capital" (James Parkes, conversation with author).

some kind of meritorious punitiveness. But "nemesis" is also linked to fate; it implies a condition that cannot be conquered.

Unlike "nemesis," the concept "antisemitism" is not ambiguous. The root of the English word does lack preciseness, but the meaning of the word is anything but imprecise. In *The Random House Dictionary* the sole definition of "antisemite" is "a person who is hostile to Jews." I would only suggest adding the qualifying words, "because they are Jews." That Arabs are reputedly a Semitic people lessens in no way the potential power of antisemitism among them. A certain German word is not readily subject to semantic game-playing: *Judenfeindschaft,* enmity toward Jews. One favorite deception of antisemites is to claim that there is no such thing as antisemitism, or at least, that if anyone is guilty of it, *they* certainly are not. If some people try to get us to say that the disease is rare or dying out, or that the word is to be used sparingly or with great caution, lest name-calling afflict us, we must be very much on guard. We must not hesitate to apply the terms "antisemitism" and "antisemite" whenever and wherever the facts warrant.

Seymour M. Lipset points out that "when one draws on the age-old hostility to Jews to strengthen a political position, when one gives credence to the charge of a worldwide Jewish plot to rule, when one attacks those with whom one has political and economic differences as Jews, when one implies that Jews are guilty of some primal evil, then one is guilty of anti-Semitism. . . ."[2] It is here adjudged that hostility to Jews is actualized through the charge that Jews are themselves hostile people.

II

Christian enmity toward Jews generally concentrates on the hostilities that Jews reputedly manifest toward God or the church or the human race, or all these together. Defensive church spokesmen

---

2. Seymour M. Lipset, " 'The Socialism of Fools:' The New Left Calls It 'Anti-Zionism,' But It's no Different from the Anti-Semitism of the Old Right," *The New York Times Magazine,* 3 January 1971, p. 6. Lipset indicates that in New Left and Black antisemitism the word "Zionist" is "simply a code word for Jew, just as it has become in Eastern Europe" (ibid., p. 26). Unlike some recent Arab hate-literature, current Soviet propaganda is too sophisticated to charge the existence of "an international Jewish conspiracy." It utilizes quite different terminology. It concentrates upon a "Zionist conspiracy." But the meaning and the purpose remain the same.

often protest that the term "Christian antisemitism" is self-contradictory. Idealists are usually mistaken, and here is one good case of this. In point of fact, the primary causal agent in Western antisemitism is the Christian message and the Christian church. Indeed, the causative influence of Christians and Christendom in the denigration and persecution of Jews, together with abiding Christian culpability for this crime, has become a truism of historical, psychological, and theological scholarship—so much so that those investigators who have researched and documented the case need only be mentioned by name: Willehad P. Eckert, Ernst L. Ehrlich, Edward H. Flannery, Malcolm Hay, Jules Isaac, Fadiey Lovsky, James Parkes, Léon Poliakov, Karl Thieme, Joshua Trachtenberg, et al.[3]

Antisemitism is one constant that suffuses all Christian history. Partly by way of a simple reminder respecting the data, but also for the sake of later reference, attention needs to be called to the most important publication in English upon the subject in 1970, a volume entitled *God's First Love*, by the Catholic scholar Friedrich Heer, a professor of the History of Ideas in the University of Vienna.[4] Dr.

---

3. Willehad P. Eckert and Ernst L. Ehrlich, *Judenhass—Schuld der Christen?!, Versuch eines Gesprächs* (Essen: Hans Driewer Verlag, 1964); Edward H. Flannery, *The Anguish of the Jews: Twenty-three Centuries of Anti-Semitism* (New York: The Macmillan Company, 1965); Malcolm Hay, *Europe and the Jews: The Pressure of Christendom on the People of Israel for 1900 years* (Boston: Beacon Press, 1960); Jules Isaac, *Genèse de l'Antisémitisme: Essai Historique* (Paris: Calmann Lévy, 1956), *Jésus et Israël*, 2d ed. (Paris: Fasquelle, 1959), *The Teaching of Contempt: Christian Roots of Anti-Semitism*, trans. Helen Weaver (New York: Holt, Rinehart and Winston, 1964); Fadiey Lovsky, *Antisémitisme et Mystère d'Israël* (Paris: Editions Albin Michael, 1955); James Parkes, *Antisemitism* (London: Vallentine Mitchell, 1963), *The Conflict of the Church and the Synagogue: A study in the origins of antisemitism* (Cleveland: World Publishing Company, 1961); Léon Poliakov, *The History of Anti-Semitism*, vol. 1 (New York: Vanguard Press, 1965); Karl Thieme, ed., *Judenfeindshaft, Darstellung und Analysen* (Frankfurt am Main: Fischer Bücherei, 1963); Joshua Trachtenberg, *The Devil and the Jews: The Medieval Conception of the Jew and its Relation to Modern Antisemitism* (Cleveland: World Publishing Company, 1961). See also Alan T. Davies, *Anti-Semitism and the Christian Mind: The Crisis of Conscience After Auschwitz* (New York: Herder and Herder, 1969); A. Roy Eckardt, *Elder and Younger Brothers: The Encounter of Jews and Christians* (New York: Charles Scribner's Sons, 1967); Charles Y. Glock and Rodney Stark, *Christian Beliefs and Anti-Semitism* (New York: Harper & Row, 1966); Rudolph M. Loewenstein, *Christians and Jews: A Psychoanalytic Study*, trans. Vera Dammann (New York: Dell Publishing Company, 1951); and Bernhard E. Olson, *Faith and Prejudice: Intergroup Problems in Protestant Curricula* (New Haven: Yale University Press, 1963).

4. Friedrich Heer, *God's First Love: Christians and Jews over Two Thousand Years*, trans. Geoffrey Skelton (New York: Weybright and Talley, 1970). The original German version appeared in 1967. For a critical analysis of this work, see the review by A. Roy Eckardt in *Commentary* 51 (March 1971): 91-98.

Heer recounts, in rather disorganized fashion but comprehensively, and in a poignant and compelling manner, the story of Christian antisemitism from its roots in the New Testament until our own day. Heer writes: "The Gospel of Jesus Christ, the 'Good News' of the Redeemer, became for millions of Jews the messenger of death. Millions of Christians have based their hatred of the Jews on it, have taken it as a call to destroy or at least enslave the Jews, 'the people who killed Christ.' "[5] In Christian Europe the "devilish, accursed race" of Jews was visited with one or more of three alternatives: death, banishment, or compulsory baptism. But we are confronted by more than ancient history. Behind the Christian world's callous indifference to the fate of Jews in the twentieth century lies an acquiescence and approval that Christians have sought "to conceal from their own conscience." It was this very indifference "that enabled Hitler to turn Europe into a graveyard of Jews."[6] Without centuries of Christian teaching and preaching against Jews, Nazism would never have been possible. The Nazi "final solution" was no more than a logical application of historic Christian attitudes and demands. Adolf Hitler could quite accurately testify that he was simply doing to the Jews what the church had counseled and acted upon for fifteen hundred years.[7] Right up to his death, Hitler "enjoyed the support of responsible leaders of both major Christian churches." He "was never excommunicated nor were his books ever placed on the Index."[8]

Some church spokesmen who are prepared to acknowledge the fact of Christian antisemitism in previous periods are not always as objective when it comes to the present. The temptation is to dismiss the evil as a thing of the past. A salient emphasis in Professor Heer's study is that the Nazi Holocaust by no means signified the end of Christian enmity to Jews. At this very moment Christian hostility to the Jewish people is manifesting itself in many and varied circles together with the propagation of teachings that perpetuate anti-semitism. Since 1945, antisemitic acts and pronouncements have been legion in lands "whose way of life has been formed by Christian principles." Heer concludes that the Christian world now looks on,

---

5. Heer, *God's First Love*, p. 22.
6. Ibid., p. 341.
7. Ibid., p. 307.
8. Ibid., pp. 296, 311.

with either indifference or approval, while a new Holocaust is planned in the Middle East.[9] The contemporaneity of Christian antisemitism will be noted later.

III

Because of the centrality of the New Testament in Christian faith, the question of the roots of antisemitism in those writings demands special attention. The Catholic theologian Rosemary Ruether asserts that the decree on the Jews of Vatican Council II was carefully framed so as to preclude "the raising of any questions" concerning antisemitic attitudes within the New Testament. She argues that antisemitism is deeply rooted in the Christian gospel of the New Testament.[10] The Catholic New Testament scholar Dominic M. Crossan is not as despairing as Dr. Ruether, but neither is he entirely happy with the Biblical documents. Crossan concludes that the term "the Jews" as employed by St. John is "a very dangerous symbolic term, and one cannot but wonder if it might be a root of anti-Semitism in the Christian subconscious."[11]

On the Protestant side, Alan T. Davies of the University of Toronto, in arguing in an important recent study *Anti-Semitism and the Christian Mind* that there is no anti-Judaism without some measure of hostility to Jews, attests that anti-Judaism inheres in any ideology that takes the New Testament to be sacrosanct, as in Protestant Biblicism. With specific reference to antisemitism, such Biblicism is held to be quite as dangerous as the persisting, dogmatic traditionalism of historic Catholicism. Passages in the New Testament that are tainted with antisemitism have been put to exactly the same antisemitic use as patristic calumnies against Jews.[12] Another

---

9. Ibid., p. 3.

10. Rosemary Ruether, "Theological Anti-Semitism in the New Testament," *The Christian Century* 85 (14 February 1968): 191-196. Cf Heer: It was "historically consistent that at the Second Vatican Council no fundamental declaration on the Jews was produced which might have led to real amends for Christian guilt towards that people" *(God's First Love*, p. 247). Subsequent events and trends within the Catholic Church have raised doubts of the complete validity of Heer's expectations.

11. Dominic M. Crossan, "Anti-Semitism and the Gospel," *Theological Studies* 26 (June 1965): 199. Crossan insists, however, that the only proper translation for John's special use of the phrase "the Jews" is "those among the authorities of the Jews who constantly opposed Jesus."

12. Davies, *Anti-Semitism and the Christian Mind,* pp. 104, 110-111, 112.

Protestant scholar, Robert E. Willis, is persuaded that until the Christian church performs acts of repentance for scriptural passages that convey anti-Judaic and antisemitic images, innuendos, and nuances, the church will continue to show that it has not been seriously affected by its continuing complicity "in the perpetuation of anti-Semitism and its nascent presence within the Christian community today. Is it too much to hope that the church might begin now to acknowledge publicly the inconsistency between the truth given in Jesus of Nazareth and those passages in the New Testament that cast aspersion on his people?"[13]

What judgment are we to make? I have never proposed the absurd conclusion that the New Testament is an antisemitic book. The very opposite is the case. Nevertheless, that antisemitic proclivities are present in the New Testament is readily seen through references to such passages as John 5:16-18; 6:41; 7:1, 13; 10:31; 19:12, 15; Acts 13:50; 20:3; and I Thessalonians 2:14-16. The fateful consideration is that all these passages, and similar ones, resort to the indiscriminate phrase "the Jews." The judgment that these passages are not free of antisemitic bias is grounded in a principle of moral philosophy. Father Gregory Baum, after conceding that the Gospel of John has often served to justify contempt for the Jewish people, nevertheless insists that the historical and religious *context* of such seemingly hostile passages forbids us to apply the word "antisemitism" to John.[14] By contrast, the principle offered here is that while the context of any proposition is relevant when discriminate or qualified judgments are tendered, the context becomes totally irrelevant when indiscriminate or unqualified judgments are being made. The truism, "some Americans are killers," is not an instance of anti-Americanism. But the indiscriminate proposition, *"the* Americans are killers," can never be redeemed through recourse to a context. The Gospel of John again and again makes indiscriminate, hostile judgments against *"the* Jews" as Jews, and this is what is meant by antisemitism. The article "the" is as decisive as the word "Jews," or more so.

---

13. Robert E. Willis, "A Perennial Outrage: Anti-Semitism in the New Testament," *The Christian Century* 87 (19 August 1970): 992.
14. Cf. Gregory Baum, *Is the New Testament Anti-Semitic?* (Glen Rock, N.J.: Paulist Press, 1965), p. 136. Baum maintains that there are no antisemitic elements in the New Testament.

The assertion "the Jews killed Jesus" (I Thess. 2:15) may be likened in structure to such a hypothetical sentence as "the Americans killed President Kennedy," containing as the latter sentence does a logical and psychological insinuation that Mr. Kennedy was not an American. So, too, the phrase "the Jews killed Jesus," which is hardly a hypothetical assertion from the standpoint of Christian detractors of Jews, insinuates that Jesus was not a Jew. It is not accidental that this very conclusion should have been eagerly drawn and perpetuated in Christian theology, a development that climaxed in the insistence of the "German Christian" movement in our century that Jesus was not Jewish but Aryan.

It need scarcely be added that as time went by during the New Testament period, the tendency was manifest to make less discriminate the category of Jewish blame respecting opposition to Jesus and the fate of Jesus.[15] How ironic it is that the more seriously the developing historical context of the New Testament is taken, the more indisputable are the evidences of *Judenfeindschaft*, indiscriminate hostility toward Jews.[16]

IV

Within Christendom antisemitism has been carried forward very largely by means of anti-Judaism and by denigration and persecution of Jews bereft of political protection. For some years these weapons have been supplemented and refined by means of anti-Zionism and/or anti-Israelism, the chief instrumentalities of contemporary Christian antisemitism.

The question is hotly debated today: Is anti-Zionism necessarily a form of antisemitism? Perhaps the answer does not always have to be "yes." To Professor Lipset, "one may oppose Israeli policy, resist Zionism or criticize worldwide Jewish support of Israel without being anti-Semitic."[17] On the other side, the presence of the State of

---

15. As examples, when Jesus symbolically destroys the Temple he is challenged by "the Jews" in John 2:18 ff., whereas in the earlier narration of this symbolic act in Mark (11:27) the challenge comes only from "the high priests, the Scribes, and the elders." Again, the cripple whom Jesus cures on the Sabbath is reproached by "the Jews" in John 5:10, whereas in the Synoptic Gospels clashes over Sabbath cures involve only the authorities (cf. Mark 3:26; Luke 6:6-11; Matt. 12:9-10, 13-14; Crossan, "Anti-Semitism and the Gospel," p. 194). In Mark "the chief priests" and "the crowd" are involved in the shout "Crucify him!" (15:11-15); in John the shouters are "the Jews" (19:15).

16. Eckardt, *Elder and Younger Brothers*, pp. 124-125; cf., more generally, pp. 122-129.

17. Lipset, " 'The Socialism of Fools,' " p. 6.

Israel as, allegedly, an aggravator of the world's woes, together with the permissiveness and even the favor accorded anti-Zionism, can certainly be used to excellent advantage by antisemites. Alan T. Davies contends that the most "fashionable contemporary guise" for antisemitism *is* anti-Zionism.[18] As Davies expresses it, antisemitic convictions "can be transposed without much difficulty into the new language of anti-Zionism, as meanwhile the reality of a Jewish nation-state offers a tangible scapegoat."[19] The antisemites often appear, therefore, to "have it made"; they can emphatically protest their complete innocence of any charge of hostility to Jews as Jews. A tried and true strategem of the devil is to convince as many as possible that he does not exist.

An analytical criterion for grappling with the relation of anti-Zionism to antisemitism has already been put forward. Insofar as anti-Zionists manifest hostility to Jews—and particularly, of course, to the Jews of Israel—there is no rational or scientific choice but to identify them as antisemites. Seymour Lipset reports that recent attacks in France upon Jews, Judaism, and Israel have diffused from the student New Left to different Catholic groups which "deny the historic claims of the Jews to Israel on the theological grounds that the church, rather than contemporary Jewry, is the true heir of ancient Israel."[20] Here is suggested a clue to the identification of anti-Israelism as a newer form of antisemitism. One measure of the presence or absence of antisemitism lies in the question: Is the integrity of the State of Israel being honored?

On 10 May 1970 a conference of Christians meeting in Beirut, Lebanon demanded the total "disappearance of Zionist structures," a euphemism for the destruction of Israel. Was this an instance of antisemitism? Well, before 1948 it may have been possible to question the practical wisdom, feasibility, or perhaps even the legitimacy of the reestablishment of a sovereign Jewish state in Palestine without being charged with antisemitism. We live almost a generation later. The assertion that Jewry has no right to Eretz Yisrael, and therefore, by implication, that the State of Israel ought to be abolished, is an instance of antisemitism. This conclusion is a

18. Davies, *Anti-Semitism and the Christian Mind*, p. 182.
19. Alan T. Davies, "Anti-Zionism, Anti-Semitism and the Christian Mind," *The Christian Century* 87 (19 August 1970): 989.
20. Lipset, " 'The Socialism of Fools'," p. 26.

perfectly objective one. There is simply no way to call for the destruction of Israel without support for a new Holocaust, the suffering and death of as many as two and one-half million Jews.[21]

V

In Christian circles, a dishonoring of the rightful integrity of Israel is not limited to categorical opposition to her continued existence. Implicit or explicit alliance with those who would harass Israel, or keep her in a threatened or insecure position, or ensure that Israel receives the short end of any political settlement, constitutes additional exemplification of hostility to the Jewish people. Particularly ominous are cases where the hostility is hidden by a third party's protestations of devotion to justice for both sides. A formidable illustration here is the recent international Quaker statement of 35,000 words entitled *Search for Peace in the Middle East.*[22] The statement is indicative of the impossibility of separating anti-Israelism and anti-Zionism from antisemitism. The Friend's judgments are by no means atypical of what we have been getting from Christian quarters; their pronouncement has received considerable attention and acclaim beyond Quaker circles, and it is often described, revealingly, as "fairminded." The Friends are reputed to stand for peace; a close inspection of their pronouncement raises the question of the continuing accuracy of the reputation.[23]

---

21. Alice and Roy Eckardt, *Encounter With Israel: A Challenge to Conscience* (New York: Association Press, 1970), pp. 217-218.

22. Two editions of the statement have been published, both under the title *Search for Peace in the Middle East.* The first was published in May 1970 by the American Friends Service Committee, Philadelphia. A slightly revised edition was published in November 1970 by the Fawcett World Library, New York, by arrangement with the American Friends Service Committee. In note 23 below, cited page references are from the revised edition.

23. A careful study of the document by the chairman of the Committee on Israel of the American Jewish Congress, Judge Justine Wise Polier, shows that it contains deep-seated anti-Jewish bias (cf. Justine Wise Polier, "Open Letter to the 'Friends,' " *Congress bi-Weekly* 37 [4 December 1970]: 3-6). This may be specifically drawn from: (1) The backing of one side in the Arab-Israeli conflict while denying that such is the case. Again and again the Friends range themselves on the Arab side and against Israel on specific issues (pp. 45, 47, 48, 72-82, 87, 97, 99-100). (2) Resort to a double standard, particularly the making of demands upon Israel that are not made of the Arabs. While accusing the Israelis of inflexibility, they give honor to Arab inflexibility (pp. 87, 99, 187). (3) A shocking reversion to historic religious bigotry and a resurrection of the conspiratorial charge against Jews. The Friends inform us that the Israelis have practiced "two-eyes-for-an-eye" retaliation (p. 31). (4) Distortions, half-truths, out-and-out falsehoods. For example, the writers make no distinction whatsoever between terror as an entrenched, long-standing, and perfectly accepted policy within Arab society, and terror as an exceptional Israeli act of the past. (5) Omissions and suppression of data (e.g., the role of the Soviet Union in the Middle East). (6) The repeated practice within cited materials of phrasing pure allegations in such a way as to make them appear to be unquestioned facts; for example, the claim that until Jewish "injustice is admitted, both by the victorious Israelis and by the international community," steps toward peace are out of the question (pp. 24, 56, 67-68, 94).

Another contemporary Christian document, which comes from a quite different source and is directed to quite different purposes from the Quaker study, is a statement adopted by the General Synod of the Nederlandse Hervormde Kerk (Reformed Church of Holland) on 16 June 1970, and entitled *Israel: People, Land and State.*[24] This document is much more traditionalist than the Friends' pronouncement, in that it contains considerably more anti-Judaism than it does explicit anti-Zionism or anti-Israelism. The Dutch Synod lives at a different end of the theological spectrum from the Quakers, yet the Dutch statement reflects much of the same bias that permeates the Quaker statement and, together with the latter, its thrust is anti-Israel.[25]

In many places the Dutch pronouncement merely repeats the classical anti-Judaist sentiments of historic Christendom. We are instructed that Jesus "came into diametrical opposition to the 'pious' ones who tried to ensure and maintain the continued existence of the

24. The version of *Israel: People, Land and State* here referred to is a mimeographed English translation made available under date of October 1970 to the Department of Faith and Order, National Council of the Churches of Christ in the U.S.A. In the analysis that follows, all references are to paragraph numbers of the document.

25. One can note also the Synod's refusal in one place to extend the integrity of the elected people's land to their right to an independent state and even to the City of Jerusalem (par. 13)—a refusal that reappears elsewhere in the effort to apply God's promise to "the lasting tie of people and land, but not in the same way to the tie of people and state" (par. 43). Despite their relative sanctioning of the Israeli state, the Dutch authors continue to "wonder" whether "the special place of the Jewish people" does not make questionable "the right of existence of the state of Israel" (par. 44). This curious disjunction between residency and sovereignty can only play into the hands of those who would have the Jews remain a (tolerated) minority devoid of independent political protection. Again, we are told that the land has been "allotted to this people in order that they might realize their vocation as God's people to form a holy society" (par. 11). The implication is all too evident that decisive Jewish irresponsibility respecting such a society may necessitate punitive expulsion from the land. The corruptness of such an outlook is attested by the fact that we never talk or act this way respecting Egypt, Syria, or Jordan. For Christians to expect from Jews, as does this pronouncement, more than is expected from other peoples (par. 52) is not only immoral, in light of the history of Christian treatment of Jews; the Synod's demand that the State of Israel be "exemplary" (par. 47) constitutes a wholly illicit intrusion of faith into the moral-political realm. This Dutch Reformed statement, together with the Quaker document, perpetuates a practice that runs all through Christian history and despoils the secular domain: the refusal to apply to the Jewish people the very same standards that are applied to all men simply because they are human beings. The Dutch pronouncement undertakes a politico-moral comparison between Israel and what it calls "Christian states," when in fact the only comparison that is legitimate is one between Israel and the states that now surround her. In the presence of foes committed to the obliteration of Israel, the Synod's expressed fear that the Jews will make their dwelling place "into a nationalistic state in which the only thing that counts is military power" (par. 48) is a moral outrage. If these churchmen are really so worried about Israeli militarism, they had better address themselves to the culprits: the Arab states, the terrorists, and the Soviet Union. The church really ought to stop lecturing Israel as though church spokesmen were Biblical prophets.

chosen people by faithful observance of the law." We are told that Jesus "repudiated those who wanted to restore national independence and who in this way strove for the self-preservation of their people" (par. 22). We are advised that "the Jewish people as a whole" rejected Jesus Christ, "their Messiah" (pars. 20, 28, 30, etc.). We are informed that "zeal for the law" was the reason for this rejection (par. 35). We are warned against "the moralism and legalism into which the observance of the law has often degenerated among the Jews" (par. 39).

Spokesmen within Jewry may succeed in propagating or opposing the doctrine of the election of Israel. That is their obligation. But whenever Christian representatives intervene in that doctrine, declaring, as does the Dutch Synod, that the Jews are "unlike" all other peoples, the specter of immorality is raised.

Even more reprehensibly, we are told again and again that the Jewish people are alienated from God (pars. 30-31, etc.), and indeed that the very Jewish act of taking refuge from death through a return to Eretz Yisrael exemplifies this alienation (par. 36). I think that a special delight of the devil must be to mete out theological-moral chastisement as the appropriate, historical sequel to human agony. That in this day after Auschwitz a Christian body should dare to stress over and over the religious alienation of the Jews is more than an instance of human callousness. It is proof that the voice of the church is sometimes a satanic voice.

Often Christians today are simply powerless to deliver themselves from traditional Christian immorality respecting the Jewish people and Judaism. Why is this? The Dutch Synod's captivity to Biblicism provides part of the answer. Unconscious Biblicism is still regnant in much of the Christian world. Moral outrages against Jews will continue to occur as long as Christendom engages in the politics of Biblicist moralism. For the Biblicist theologization of politics is a guarantor of immorality. In the case under review, this consequence is particularly ironic because these Dutch churchmen are doubtless reacting, and commendably so, against the terrible divorce of theology from politics in the Europe, and especially the Germany, of the 1930s and 1940s.

Most horrendous of all is the truth that the very Christian world that has brought incalculable suffering to Jews should continue to spawn representatives who make the same old accusations against the Jewish people and the same old impossible demands upon them. Sadly, these representatives' are often well-meaning Christians and humanitarians, committed to "the highest moral values." Of one thing we may be quite certain: The Quakers who wrote the one statement and the Dutch Christians who wrote the other would in all honesty resent the charge that they are antisemites.

VI

How are we to account for this horror, this antisemitism that has afflicted the Christian church throughout her history, and that endures to this day? How is the evil to be rooted out or at least reduced? Each of these two questions is as baffling as the other. A lifetime of study may uncover a few clues, though perhaps no demonstrable certainties.

At the outset, some necessarily personal references will perhaps be excused. For some time I have sought to till soil that is shared by depth psychology, theology, and ethics: antisemitism is the war we Christians wage against Jesus the Jew; the reenactment of the crucifixion of Christ, who confronts Christians with God; the rejection of the Jew Jesus turned against his own people.[26] As Friedrich Heer puts it: The Jew Jesus is to blame; the Jew has to be repressed.[27] Through our persecution of Jews we Christians can try to manage our guilt for defaulting before gospel demands.

While this (somewhat eclectic) position is not to be discarded, one may come to wonder whether God and man are the only leading protagonists in the revolting drama, or whether the devil is not also at center stage. I think that I never really began to take the devil with seriousness until I had developed what some of my critics regard as an obsession with antisemitism. Even so, my reflections upon the devil were not initiated until fairly recently.

To put the matter as circumspectly as possible, one cannot come to grips with the reality of Christian antisemitism, and hence of Christian hostility to Israel, without acknowledging the reality of satanic forces. Opponents will perhaps identify this development as a predictable culmination of years of unjust and misguided warfare on my part: the last resort of the fanatic is to charge that the other is consorting with the devil. The risk of this kind of interpretation is simply one that has to be taken. (I am sometimes sent to the edge of despair by the fear that my endless preaching upon the fact of Christian antisemitism may, devilishly, serve to compound the evil.)

When the devil enters, what happens to the concept and the reality of nemesis? Upon whom is retribution visited? What becomes of responsibility? What of the future? What is to be the fate of fate?

---

26. Eckardt, *Elder and Younger Brothers*, pp. 22-25.
27. Heer, *God's First Love*, p. 424.

So far, I hypothesize that Satan's major field of operations is the collective unconscious. In Christian antisemitism certain eruptions of the collective unconscious are taken captive by pathology. The pathology assumes a unique form, since it is different from ordinary racial or ethnic prejudice. The utilization of the Christian pulpit to defame Blacks or Germans, or even Russians, has, indeed, become quite unfashionable. Yet we shall continue to read the "Word of God" in, for example, the Gospel of John—and no one had better summon the Anti-Defamation League. Who wishes to be accused of undermining "religious freedom"?

Further, even though Professor Lipset has been cited above in support of the judgment that antisemitic hostility is actualized through the claim that Jews are themselves hostile or evil people, this judgment must not obscure the truth that antisemitism has a profound life of its own quite independent of the presence or behavior of Jews. In its depths, antisemitism has little if anything to do with Jews. It lives in the mind of the devil, the antisemite. This is why it is that changes in Jewish behavior are of no consequence in the presence of antisemitism. Only antisemitism demands that certain human beings be angels yet insists that they are devils. Just as the reality of the devil is to be unreal, so antisemitism is immured to reality. Anti-Israeli Christians need have little if any connection with Jews or with the real Israel. They fabricate their own Israel: militant, aggressive, inflexible, vengeful, irreligious, alienated.

Is antisemitism simply one among many of the devil's enterprises, or is it a special malignancy that works to destroy the whole divine-human creation? David Polish contends that "the truth of every cause is validated or found fraudulent in the way in which it confronts the Jewish people."[28] It is not impossible that the world will reach its end by courtesy of the Middle East.

The reign of the Lord extends to all men, yet he chooses his elect nation. The dominion of the devil is also universalistic—his kingdom is indiscriminate—yet he too has his chosen ones, the antisemites. He does not leave himself without special witnesses. Through the centuries and in all places his faithful persist. The universality transcends the particularity, yet it is realized *through* the particularity: Jews are hated without boundaries of time or place. The

---

28. David Polish, "The Tasks of Israel and Galut," *Judaism* 28 (Winter 1969): 10.

devil is universal yet very particular. As Friedrich Heer points out, the Christian theologians proved Jewish guilt a thousand times.[29]

The "two-eyes-for-an-eye" Christian psyche calls down retribution upon the allegedly evil Jew for rejecting the divine light—an "inner light," perhaps, to our friends the Friends. To them, the refusal of Jews to surrender themselves like good pacifists must be an unforgiveable sin against some kind of Holy Ghost. Yet upon whom is the final retribution falling?

Why is it incumbent upon us to identify Christian antisemites as specially chosen legions of the devil? Because Christianity long ago arranged a pact with the demonic forces. The devil can only be known by his fruits. The antisemites of Christian history and of this moment whisper their secret to us: The Jews are the devil, the devil is the Jews. "Psychologically and morally construed, the charge of Jewish devilishness demonstrates the satanic conquest of the Christian soul. The Christian is the 'Jew' he despises. I would even go so far as to say that the Jew is in fact the 'Christian': Jewish ideals and behavior are the polar opposite of the church's accusations. The Jewish world-conspiracy is the invention of demon-ridden Christian conspirators."[30]

VII

Can there be, then, any real hope for the conquest of Christian antisemitism? A collective-pathological state such as the one under analysis cannot be separated from either the idealism that demands perfection or the cynicism that awaits nothing good. Idealism and cynicism are common flights from the real world. But the Jew is *here*. He is the world, he is reality. The only end to antisemitism is a revolutionary restoration of reality. Yet is there a chance for any such development? Someone may interject that the cynicism implied in this very question must itself be pathological. Perhaps so. If Elie Wiesel is right, ours is the time when only madmen may be sane. But I believe that we are not yet so far gone that we cannot distinguish between pathological cynicism and the cynicism that is an objective and reasonable response to the fatefulness of the pathology.

---

29. Heer, *God's First Love*, p. 324.
30. Eckardt, review of Heer, *God's First Love*, in *Commentary*, p. 94.

Christianity means antisemitism; this is the dreadful truth that overwhelms us once more as we close such a volume as Friedrich Heer's agonized chronicle. Yet, Professor Heer does not surrender hope. Christianity can yet redeem itself, he tells us—by surmounting its Augustinian contempt for the world and returning home to its Jewish foundation, where men are responsible partners of God and earthly love is accepted and incarnated.

I should love to share this expectation. There are, however, formidable stumblingblocks. The affirmation that Christianity ought to be Jewish at its very roots may only make for a metastasizing of antisemitism—although I have often made that affirmation myself (sometimes out of desperation). Heer pleads that Christians accept their guilt, and then through a massive act of self-analysis purge themselves of their sins. One serious difficulty is that to suggest to Christians that they may be antisemitic can quite likely make them more antisemitic. Were it not for the Jew—they may secretly tell themselves—no one could ever go around making the charge of antisemitism against them. Indeed, the very raising of the issue of Christian guilt sometimes proves counterproductive. Professor Davies points out that even minor Christian guilt feelings over Auschwitz

produce a curious reaction: one is tempted to conclude that it comes almost as a relief to [Christians] to discover that Jews, like Christians, are capable of wrongdoing. The frequent journalistic comparisons between Zionist militarism and nazi militarism are instructive at this point. To find Israel in a morally ambiguous situation releases the Christian from thinking too much about Auschwitz and his own vicarious participation in one of the darkest moments of Western history. It is as if the Christian conscience whispers: "See, we aren't that bad after all—look at what the Jews are doing now!" Such an attitude, conscious or unconscious, is doubly bad. It is bad because it makes the Christian psychologically vulnerable to anti-Semitism as well as to anti-Zionism, and it is bad because it deflects the church from its own sins by concentrating on the sins of others.[31]

However, the real nemesis is that Friedrich Heer's program may have come too late. The church that collaborated in the Nazi "final solution" dealt itself mortal blows. From that Jewish crucifixion and Christian self-crucifixion there could and did come a Jewish resurrection—the State of Israel—but not a Christian resurrection.

31. Davies, "Anti-Zionism, Anti-Semitism and the Christian Mind," p. 989.

For the church has nowhere to go now. Christianity is Cain, a fugitive upon the face of the earth. The fateful and all-decisive consideration is that the church of the "final solution" was simply living out to an ultimate fulfillment its own historical fate. For Christian antisemitism was born at the moment of God's first death. How, then, is antisemitism to die unless there is a new resurrection, the birth of a fresh God?

VIII

We are confronted, finally, by a grave moral danger: a realization of the nemesis of amassing prophetic judgments against the Christian community may combine with our terrible knowledge of Christianity's demise to make us abandon the struggle against Christian antisemitism. Does the death of Christianity force the Christian to betray his Christian identity? It is a blessing that we know so little of the battles that rage in heaven. We are ignorant of just what intentions God has for the devil. Consequently, we can see ourselves as free. We are responsible men. We have to fight against our own nemesis, lest sin gain the one victory it yet must covet, our final consent.

One battle for today has to be waged against the maneuver by either hidden or unconscious antisemites—or perhaps by well-meaning "liberals" who wish to bury the past for the sake of mutual Jewish-Christian acceptance in the present—to bar the subject of past and present Christian antisemitism from primary study and analysis. This can only mean cutting off the possibility of penitence and corrective action. Harvey Cox writes: "Psychiatrists have long reminded us that the loss of the sense of time is a symptom of personal deterioration. . . . The same is true for a civilization. So long as it can absorb what has happened to it and move confidently toward what is yet to come, its vitality persists." But alienation from its past means decline and ultimately death.[32] The tacit pretense that history never happened does not, unfortunately, ever make history go away. It simply is not true that the Christian world as a whole has ever repented of its antisemitic actions and attitudes. Yet the church will hardly change her behavior effectively or enduringly

---

32. Harvey Cox, *Feast of Fools* (Cambridge: Harvard University Press, 1969), p. 12.

until she faces up to her past and present sins.

There appears no way to work through or with self-defensive Christians who resent or at least oppose any raising of the issue of continuing Christian responsibility for antisemitism. Are we left, then, with nothing to say to Christians today who honestly feel no guilt for antisemitism? Much depends upon whether they consider themselves an integral, and therefore in a sense a responsible, part of the total Christian community. In other words, it may be asked whether these Christians have any really deep sense of their own history. At the very least, Christians ought to ask themselves whether a denial of any genuine responsibility for antisemitism is a morally justified conclusion, or whether it is in fact a temptation not unrelated to the machinations of the devil.

Is there a path out of the cynicism that is the ineluctable outcome of our own history? Is there any way for the Christianity that killed itself to be raised from the dead? Perhaps one hope for the future lies with that remnant of Christians who do not directly bear guilt for Christian antisemitism but who may be called to wage war upon a past that remains as yet unmastered *(eine unbewältigte Vergangenheit)*. Youth of today are expending wonderful energy in behalf of many social causes. They seek to redeem the past, a past that carries many evils for which they are obviously not subject to blame. Christian students and other young people in this country may be challenged by such an enterprise as the German Reconciliation Movement *(Aktion Sühnezeichen)*. Teams of German youth give up paid employment for a year in order to engage in deeds of construction within various European and Middle Eastern countries, to the end of forgiveness for the crimes of their fellow-countrymen against Jews and other "enemies" of the Third Reich. The overwhelming moral fact here is that the great majority of the participants in *Aktion Sühnezeichen* were not even born when World War II started. No one can accuse them of perpetrating the Nazi program against Jews. The penitence of these young people is entirely vicarious; they have taken upon themselves the sins of the fathers. They would be the first to grant that their efforts are not free from a wish for national self-respect and even from an element of self-interest. The plain truth stands that they are actively engaged in the search for human reconciliation. Who in fact builds for the future—the man who desires to bury the past, refusing to allow any real link between his present behavior and that past, or the man who dedicates himself to redeeming the present consequences of the past?[33]

Beyond Christianity and the nemesis of the Christian's own condition stand God and his people. We are left with a choice between hope and despair. I wish, in the end, to testify on the side of hope. Why do I do this? Because the Jewish people do not give in to us, who have been the devil. They do not give in to hatred. At the last we may join with Friedrich Heer: Perhaps God will live once more, not so much because of us, but because he is "the coming God: a God of the present and of the future, in which he will submerge the brutal past."[34]

33. A. Roy Eckardt, "Christian Guilt," *Christian News From Israel* (Jerusalem) 28 (July 1967): 47-48.
34. Heer, *God's First Love*, p. 444.

PART TWO

CONTEMPORARY JUDAISM

IN THEOLOGICAL PERSPECTIVE

Rabbinic Foundations of Modern Jewish Thought

SEYMOUR SIEGEL

When I use the term Rabbinic, I mean the Talmudic and Rabbinic literature which was created by the Jewish people somewhere between the second or third century before the Christian era until the sixth century of the Christian era when the Talmudic literature was officially closed, though unofficially it continues until this day.

There is a famous story told in the Talmud[1] about Moses, who, when he went up to Heaven to receive the Torah, the Revelation, found God putting jots and tittles on the letters of scripture, and he asked the Almighty, "What are you doing? Why are you bothering to put these jots and tittles on letters that are soon to become sacred writ?" The Almighty replied that in future generations there would be a great scholar whose name is Rabbi Akiba—the greatest of the teachers of the Talmud—and that he, through his talent, inspiration, and wisdom, would be able to derive mountains of laws, and teachings even from the jots and tittles on the letters. "Therefore," said God, "I am doing it for his benefit." Moses was intrigued by this answer of the Almighty and said, "I would like very much, if possible, to sit in on a lecture given by Rabbi Akiba."

Of course, here on earth it would be impossible to put time ahead several thousand years, but in Heaven everything is possible; and so, according to the Rabbinic story, Moses was given a seat in the back row of Rabbi Akiba's academy, which really met in the second century of the Christian era. He listened intently to what was being taught by Rabbi Akiba, but could not understand a word of what was being said. Of course, Moses was upset by this experience. Finally, as Rabbi Akiba's lecture continued, Akiba said, "Everything that I have just lectured about comes as a result of the Torah given by Moses." When Moses heard this, he was reconciled and his anxiety

---

1. *Menachot*, 29b.

and discomfort vanished.

This story, which was probably told by the rabbis to make fun of their own ingenuity, illustrates an important aspect of Judaism which is at the very core of the understanding of Jewish faith and way of life. Judaism is the result of an ongoing process starting from the Bible and continuing through the ages. This process, which is the confrontation and the dialogue between the texts of the past and the needs and understandings of the present, is really in the spirit of those who founded the religion of Israel, even though they themselves, including Moses, the greatest of all, might not recognize its contours as it developed through the ages.[2]

One of the greatest heresies in contemporary and even ancient Judaism is to be a "Biblical" Jew, i.e., being solely a Biblical Jew. Though in Judaism the Biblical and Rabbinic periods are classic and are the ground out of which the faith has grown, they do not represent the last and final expression of Judaism. Jewish faith is an ongoing experience of the Jewish people as they live in the presence of God, and with the realization of their destiny as the people of the covenant.

This process of renewing the ancient text in the light of present reality and understanding is called in classical Hebrew vocabulary *Midrash*, a Hebrew word deriving from the root *Derash*, which means to search, to plumb the depths of the text and of the tradition.[3] It is this process of Midrash more than any other theological principle which characterizes the structure of Judaism from its Rabbinic elaboration until the present day. It is the process of Midrash which makes the ancient text live anew and receive new vitality even under circumstances that were unprecedented and unforeseen by those who first laid the foundations of Judaism.

The importance of the category of Midrash cannot be over-estimated. It represents the hinge upon which the whole entity of Judaism turns. It is no accident that Spinoza, the first great modern Jew and the first great modern Jewish heretic, probably the arch-heretic of all modern Judaism, attacked first of all this whole process of Midrash and said it is illicit and not warranted by

2. See Solomon Schechter's introduction in his *Studies in Judaism: First Series* (Philadelphia: Jewish Publication Society of America, 1911).
3. See George Foot Moore, *Judaism in the First Centuries of the Christian Era: The Age of the Tannaim*, 2 vols. (Cambridge, Mass.: Harvard University Press, 1954), 1:56-82.

philosophy.[4]

Two well-known examples of the way this process of Midrash worked in Rabbinic times and in contemporary Judaism as well may be offered. Everyone is acquainted with the famous verse in the Bible which calls for "an eye for an eye," and to many this is the characteristic approach of what people call the Old Testament. When they say "old" testament, they mean a primitive approach in relationship to development in religion in later centuries.

Incidentally, modern scholarship has shown that even an eye for an eye, the technical or literal *lex talionis*, was a tremendous advance over the pagan notion of several eyes for one eye. In the Talmud and the Midrash, it is explained that the verse "an eye for an eye" is properly to be understood not as referring to the *lex talionis*, the law of retribution in which the aggressor's organ is treated in the same fashion in which he treated his victim. Rather it is to be understood as calling for monetary compensation.

The argument of the rabbis is a very interesting one.[5] They argued that it is impossible literally to apply the law of an eye for an eye, since no two eyes are equal, either in size or acuity of vision. Assume that I have a twenty-twenty vision and you have a twenty-forty vision, and through some aggression I happen to knock out your eye. If you take out mine, it really is not an eye for an eye. Therefore, even if the aggressor's eye were to be removed in punishment, this would not fulfill literally the Biblical injunction if you were to take it literally. Thus they say that the intention of the lawgiver was not to call for retribution and retaliation, but rather to ordain monetary payment for the damage which had been inflicted upon the unfortunate victim.

This Midrash, it would seem clear to most of us, does not literally express the intent of the lawgiver. Nevertheless the rabbis ordained through their understanding and through their Midrash that "an eye for an eye" should be understood as calling for monetary compensation rather than the retaliation which seems to be the literal meaning of the verse. Since that time, this is the way Jewish practice and understanding has followed the meaning of the text.

Another illustration of the power and the range of the Midrashic method as applied to the tradition of Israel can be understood from

---

4. See Leo Strauss, *Spinoza's Critique of Religion* (New York: Schocken Books, 1965).
5. *B. Babba Kamma*, 84a.

an example as to how the Rabbinic authorities deal with the idea of war, or the Hebrew word *Milchama,* as it is sometimes mentioned in scripture. There is a verse in the Song of Songs in which the "bed of Solomon" is described as being surrounded by "sixty brave warriors, all of them holding swords and schooled in the ways of war." In the Rabbinic period, Jewish leaders could not conceive of the glorification of a military hero nor could they understand why anybody's bed had to be surrounded by sixty heroes, as they themselves had long abandoned the profession of the soldier. They said that when the Bible refers to the retinue which surrounded the bed of Solomon as learned in the ways of war, it really had reference to the war of the Torah. It does not mean a holy war; it means the discussion of the Torah, the analytical and dialectical process by which the true meanings of the ancient text are established. According to the Rabbinic picture, King Solomon had these sixty scholars in a symposium, and they would discuss the intricacies of scripture and tradition. That is what is meant by Milchama as war; namely, the scholarly and analytical controversies that arise when people talk about important things.

These two examples should suffice to illustrate the literally thousands of interpretations and understandings which are the result of Rabbinic Midrash. It is also important to point out that this process of Midrash did not stop with the Rabbinic period, but that it continued throughout the ages, reaching very substantial heights during the Middle Ages when an entirely new Midrash was created in reference to the Torah. In the schools of the scholastic philosophers, many of the texts of Judaism were reinterpreted in the light of their understanding. Thus, Abraham Heschel has remarked that Judaism is "a minimum of revelation and a maximum of interpretation."[6]

After having set down this foundation, it is necessary also to deal with other foundations of Rabbinic Judaism which persist until the present time and which represent the setting for any contemporary understanding of Jews and their religion. The main foundation, the root of all roots, is God, Who is professed and acknowledged as active in history and Who is the God of Israel and the God of all men; Who is both close and far, imminent and transcendent; Who is called *Avinu* and *Malkenu,* our Father and our King; Who is closer

---

6. Abraham Joshua Heschel, *God in Search of Man* (Philadelphia: Jewish Publication Society, 1963), p. 274.

than any other reality and whose abode is the highest of high heavens and whose glory is greater than any imagination of the mind of man.[7]

God is worshipped in the midst of life. He is not found in ecstatic trances or in transcendental meditation, rather, He is in the very midst of the struggles and hopes and failures of man. The Talmud does tell us of a rather ill-fated voyage which four Rabbinic scholars made into "Pardes" (Paradise), which is interpreted as meaning a mystical and ecstatic experience. Of the four who made that voyage, one became mad; one died; one became a heretic; and it was only Rabbi Akiba who was able to make that voyage. But he only made it once; for once was enough.[8]

It is interesting at this point to interpolate a very pregnant statement made by Martin Buber in reply to Aldous Huxley's call for a pursuit of religious experience in consciousness-expanding drugs. Buber wrote, "In reality, the consumer of Mescalin does not emerge from this net into some sort of free participation in common being, rather merely into a strictly private special sphere given to him as his own for several hours. The chemical holidays of which Huxley speaks are holidays not only from the petty I enmeshed in the machinery of its aims, but also from the person participating in the community of logos and cosmos, holidays from the very uncomfortable reminder to verify one's self as such a person."[9] That is to say, the psychedelic experience, whatever it is, is not a true religious experience because it is not an experience of the divine within the world as it is, but is a chemical holiday. This is the Biblical, Rabbinic, and, I presume, also the normative Christian view regarding the confrontation and encounter between the human and the divine.

Max Kadushin has given the normative religious experience, which Rabbinic Judaism tries to induce in its devotees, the name "normal mysticism."[10] This term means that the believer, or more correctly the one who lives Judaism, experiences the divine through his everyday activity and does not require abnormal states of being,

7. See Solomon Schechter, *Some Aspects of Rabbinic Theology* (New York: Macmillan Co., 1909), pp. 21-96.
8. *B. Chagiga*, 14b. See also Gershom G. Scholem, *Major Trends of Jewish Mysticism*, 3d ed. (New York: Schocken Books, 1954), pp. 78-79.
9. Martin Buber, *The Knowledge of Man* (New York: Harper Torchbooks, 1965), p. 100.
10. Max Kadushin, *The Rabbinic Mind* (New York: Jewish Theological Seminary, 1952), pp. 194ff.

psychedelic journeys or mystical illumination in order to feel an experience before the divine. This is achieved, as we will soon see, through the observance of the Halakha, the law, and through the notion that although the world itself is not God, it is His creation; and therefore by working and living in the world we are living in the presence of the creator of the world.[11]

The God of the rabbis is no abstraction, no principle, not a being with a capital B, but a Person Whom one encounters in the very midst of living, in eating, in playing, in working, and of course, in studying. This is embodied in the most original creation of Rabbinic liturgical production, namely, the *Berakha* or the blessing,[12] which all Jews are commanded to recite before partaking of food, before studying, and before engaging in the various activities of life. Through the Berakha we invoke the presence of God and recognize it even in the midst of mundane activities.

Study takes on more than an intellectual quality. Whereas in prophetic times God reached down to man and touched the mind and the soul of the prophets, the rabbis ordained—practically commanded—that prophecy cease. They said that prophecy had ceased with the death of Zechariah, Haggai, and Malachi. Through study and learning, we go up to the Divine. Through learning, a ladder will be built whose foundation will be upon the earth and whose head will reach into the heavens themselves. Not only is learning important to get to God but, according to the Rabbinic view, God himself sets aside part of his day for study. He studies the Torah like anyone else does. In the Rabbinic view, sometimes he is even wrong in his conclusions and he corrects them in reference to what the academies below decide. This God is a God of steadfastness who is both the Lord of Nature, the Lord of all Humankind, and the God of Israel, too.

There is an interesting law in the Talmud which I think illustrates this concept. In the Mishna—the basis of the Talmud—it is written that he who prays about something which has already happened engages in a *Tefillat Shav,* a vain prayer.[13] Two examples are given of these vain prayers. If a man is going into a city and sees great excitement resulting from a fire that is consuming some house, he

11. Schechter, *Some Aspects of Rabbinic Theology,* pp. 21-45.
12. On the Berakha, see Kadushin, *The Rabbinic Mind,* pp. 202ff.
13. *Mishna Berakot,* chap. 9.

should not say, "I pray that it is not my house which is on fire," because common sense would show that the prayer cannot change what has already happened. The house is already burning and his prayer cannot change the fact that it is his or not his. Another example: If a man's wife is already pregnant, he should not pray that the child be born a son (being male chauvinists, they could not conceive of anybody praying that the child should be a daughter), because the sex of the child, according to his own biology and ours too, has already been determined. Therefore it is useless to appeal to God to change a fact that is already existent. These two examples show that the rabbi's understanding of God as the Lord of Nature is such that he is reliable in the way nature runs, sustains it in its custom, and is therefore steadfast. But also, he is available in encounter and in prayer and, above all, in study.

The second foundation of Rabbinic Judaism which persists until this day, and which perhaps is even more important than the first, is a self-understanding of the people of Israel as the people of the covenant.[14] This is, as in the Bible, the central category by means of which the people of Israel understands itself.[15] Covenant is a principle through which the community of Israel sees itself not as a people as all other peoples, or as a religious society promoting some principle or idea, but as a group in relationship to God.

The covenant has as its goal the promotion of justice and truth in man's corporate and individual life; and the covenant requires, or at least has its genesis in, a land where the obligation of the covenant may be experienced and observed. Thus the covenant with the people of Israel is also made immediately with the land of Israel.[16]

Celebration of the importance of Israel does not result in exclusivism. It was the Israelites in the Talmudic period who taught the principle of the seven Noahide commandments by means of which the righteous of all the world have a share in the world to come. There is a kind of general covenant made with all mankind, the content of which are the seven commandments of basic natural religion and ethics. While the children of Israel live under a special

---

14. Schechter, *Some Aspects of Rabbinic Theology*, pp. 46ff.
15. See Walther Eichrodt, *Theology of the Old Testament*, trans. J. A. Baker, 2 vols. (Philadelphia: Westminster Press, 1961-1967).
16. See Abraham Joshua Heschel, *Israel, An Echo of Eternity* (New York: Farrar, Straus and Giraux, 1969), pp. 43-93.

covenant and have additional responsibilities, both Jew and non-Jew share in the covenant with God through two different covenants.

The turning point in the Rabbinic period occurred in the year 70 of the Christian era, when the temple and the commonwealth were destroyed. This disaster was compounded by the ill-fated rebellion of the year 135 of the Christian era under Bar Kokhba, and the special relationship of Israel and God could not but be called into question.

There is a semi-humorous story in the Talmud[17] which apparently refers to a colloquy between a Christian and a Jew. Rabbi Joshua B. Hananiah was standing in the house of Caesar, and a certain Min, probably a Christian, showed in pantomime a people from whom God has turned his face. Rabbi Joshua showed in pantomime his hands stretched out over us. Caesar said to Rabbi Joshua, "What did he show you?" And the rabbi answered, "He showed me a people whose Lord has turned away his face from them, and I showed him his hand which is stretched out over us." As great as the catastrophe must seem, the rabbis assured the people that God was still with them; indeed, that he himself, so to speak, was suffering with them. That is an important Rabbinic principle—that God himself suffers with the sufferings of his people and of all people.[18] So when there is a catastrophe impending upon the people, a Jew is supposed to put ashes of humiliation on the Ark of the Law to signify the fact that God himself also is suffering and God himself is in exile with the people of Israel. The sufferings were seen as a testing of the people rather than a rejection. "Flax improves when threshed, but only when it is of good quality ... a potter does not have to test a cracked vessel lest it break. He tests only the perfect vessel and God, therefore, tries the righteous."[19]

The strongest challenge to the Rabbinic self-understanding of the Jewish people as a people of the covenant came with the rise of Christianity, when some authorities claimed that with the Christian covenant the Jewish covenant had been superceded. These challenges have been compounded in modern times by misguided universalists, such as George Bernard Shaw who viewed the Jewish identity of

---

17. *Hagiga*, 5B. See also Seymour Siegel, "Election and the People of God—A Jewish Perspective," *Lutheran Quarterly* 21 (December 1969): 443.
18. See Abraham Joshua-Heschel, *The Prophets* (New York: Harper and Row, 1962), pp. 221ff.
19. *Taanit*, 17a.

being a God-chosen people like the Nazi racist theory, as rooted in racial arrogance. These sentiments have also been echoed by Arnold Toynbee and others who have accused Judaism of introducing intolerance and self-centeredness into the world. To compare the Nazi idea and the Biblical and Rabbinic assertion is like comparing a monkey with a human being. There is some superficial resemblance, but the difference is more crucial than the resemblance.

The notion of covenant and of the special quality of Jewish existence and life has been most eloquently stated in contemporary Jewish thinking and writing by Emil Fackenheim of the University of Toronto, one of the leading Jewish theologians of our time. In referring to the really central and crucial event of Jewish existence in the twentieth century, that which is symbolized by the name Auschwitz (the concentration and death camp constructed by the Nazis), Fackenheim has written, "Most assuredly no *redeeming* voice is heard from Auschwitz or ever will be heard. However, a *commanding* Voice is being heard, and has, however faintly, been heard from the start. Religious Jews hear it, and they identify its source. Secularist Jews also hear it, even though perforce they leave it unidentified. At Auschwitz, Jews came face to face with absolute evil. They were and still are singled out by it, but in the midst of it, they hear an absolute commandment: *Jews are forbidden to grant posthumous victories to Hitler.* They are commanded to survive as Jews, lest the Jewish people perish."[20] This very determination to persist and survive, even if secularly motivated, is an expression of the Jewish attachment to a transcendent purpose. The very survival of the Jew is a response to a divine command. The overwhelming response of Jews to the threat of the State of Israel is testimony to that determination. Thus Will Herberg wrote in an interesting essay entitled "The 'Chosenness' of Israel" that he had yet to find a Jew who does not in some manner of form exhibit this profound sense of difference and special vocation.[21] The outcome of the covenant theology for Rabbinic Judaism is the duty and obligation to survive; and in Rabbinic eyes it is also a privilege to observe what Christians call the Law. The word Law as referring to the system of Jewish

20. Emil Fackenheim, "Jewish Faith and the Holocaust: A Fragment," *Commentary* 46 (August 1968): 32.
21. Will Herberg, "The 'Chosenness' of Israel and the Jew of Today," *Midstream* 1 (Autumn 1955): 83-91.

observance is a result of an unfortunate mistranslation perpetrated by the Septuagint Greek translators who took the word Torah and transmuted it into the word *Nomos*.

The term which Jews use is *Halacha*, the way, the way of life, which is the living out on the level of doing of the obligations of the covenant. The function of the Halacha is a regulating one, to lead Israel into the ways of God and to keep alive the moments of faith which might become evaporated in the hustle and bustle of life, thus keeping the Jew in touch with the higher reality.[22] The *Mitzvoth* (the 613 commandments derived from the Bible) were given to Israel in order to purify and refine them, in order that life should not overcome them; they should be able to sanctify life. The Law is not the end-all and be-all of Judaism, for behind the Halacha there is an obligation to do more than the law, to go beyond the rigid demands of the law. But it is the minimum Jewish obligation and the way in which the life of the covenant people is turned from the divine towards God.

Reform Judaism, which in the nineteenth century defied and challenged the notion of a Judaism based on the Halacha, has now, at least in its *avant-garde*, reformed itself to the necessity of law, though it will not be exactly the same as the traditional law. Nevertheless, it has the function and the character of Jewish observance.

Abraham Heschel has summarized all of this in these words: "Sacred deeds are designed to make living *compatible with our sense of the ineffable*. The Mitzvot are forms of expressing in deed the appreciation of the ineffable. Religion without Mitzvot is an experience without the power of expression, a sense of mystery without the power of sanctity, a question without an answer. Without Torah we have only deeds that dream of God."[23]

All of this is combined in Rabbinic literature with the nurturing of the Messianic hope which plays such an important role in Judaism and in the subsequent developments of Jewish faith and life. It is the Messianic hope which partakes of the imagination of the people. The rabbis teach that preceding the Messianic days, imprudence

---

22. Schechter, *Some Aspects of Rabbinic Theology*, p. 116.
23. Abraham Joshua Heschel, *God in Search of Man* (Philadelphia: Jewish Publication Society, 1963), p. 350.

(Chutzpah) will increase: inflation will become great; the young will not respect the old; the face of the generation will be as the face of a dog.[24] The rabbis did not believe in automatic progress in our moving toward the Messianic days; rather, they believed that the Messianic days themselves might be preceded by great catastrophes. Therefore, only the Messiah will be able to help us.

The Jewish Messianic hope is related to concrete life, the social life of nations and men. The Rabbinic view of the future is not of some spiritual exultation the individual experiences, but the hope for the return from exile of the people of Israel to the land of Israel, the coming together of men and nations in love and brotherhood, and a reconciliation of nature with God and the Cosmos with its creator. [25]

It is a Messianic hope which does not neglect the present. A famous passage in the Talmud asserts that we prepare the way for the Messiah today when we obey God's commandments. "Rabbi Yachana ben Zakkai said, 'If you have a seedling in your hand, and they say, "Look here comes the Messiah," 'plant the seedling first and then go out to meet him.' "[26] It is a turning towards the future without turning away from the present, as it is a duty to sanctify the present with a hope and an outlook toward the future. The Messianic hope of Judaism is the hope that transcends disappointments. It counsels both activism in preparing the way for the Messianic fulfillment and a patience to wait for God's own action in redeeming history even though He may tarry and may be delayed. This Rabbinic view tries to avoid the pitfalls of Utopianism, which is the announcement that the Messiah has already come when indeed he has not yet (even though people might think that the Age of Aquarius is here because the stars now have arranged themselves in a particular way), to avoid premature greeting of the Messiah, and to test all Messianic claims by social reality. Also, it avoids the pitfall of cynicism which says that nothing can be done to prepare the world for the Messianic redemption.

One of the most profound of all Rabbinic stories is that concerning one of the Rabbinic sages who found the Messiah sitting at the gates of Rome as a leprous beggar. He asked the Messiah,

---

24. *Mishna Sotah*, chap. 9:15.
25. See Louis Jacobs, *Principles of the Jewish Faith* (New York: Basic Books, 1964), pp. 368-398.
26. *Avot d'rabbi Natan* [Schechter], Recension B, chap. 31, p. 34.

"When will you come?" The Messiah said, "Today." The rabbi went back to his colleagues and joyfully proclaimed that the Messiah was soon to arrive. Of course, the day passed and the Messiah did not come. He went back to Rome and asked, "Why did you mislead me?" The Messiah referred him to the verse in Scripture which promises, "Today, if you will but hearken to my voice."[27]

These are the foundations of Jewish life today whose roots can be found in Rabbinic literature: a loyalty to the living God who encounters us within the world, demanding from us to sanctify and to overcome the dichotomies of the sacred and the profane; an identity for those who are part of the covenanted people with the destiny and grandeur of the community of Israel pledged to be a kingdom of priests and a holy people; a commitment to a sanctified life through the observance of the Halacha which keeps us in touch, not only with the rhythms of nature, but with the high points of the liturgical year and the holy events in Jewish history; and a life which is inspired by a hope which does not sell the present in order to gain the future or abandon the future in order to save the present.

The literature of the rabbis may be summarized as a plea for *Shalom,* which in Jewish literature means a good deal more than peace.[28] Shalom is God's name. It is integrity, wholeness, steadfastness, community, solidarity, and the total mobilization of human powers to serve the reality which is above and beyond us. Therefore, the central word in Rabbinic literature is the word Shalom. Consequently, it is no accident that the whole of Talmudic literature ends with that word: "The Holy One, blessed be He, could find no vessel that was so full of blessing for Israel and mankind as that of Shalom."[29]

---

27. *Sanhedrin,* 98a.
28. See Johs. Pedersen, *Israel: Its Life and Culture,* 4 vols. in 2 (London: Oxford University Press, 1926-1940), 1:263-310.
29. *Mishna, Uktzin,* 3:12.

Contemporary Jewish Theology:
Four Major Voices

SEYMOUR SIEGEL

Several years ago, a volume was published entitled *The Condition of Jewish Belief* in which thirty-eight rabbis expressed their beliefs and theological commitments. The editor of this book, Milton Himmelfarb, said, "There are few new ideas about Judaism. On the whole, therefore, the relative absence of newness was to be expected together with the dominant intellectual, if not emotional calm."[1]

There is theologizing going on in the Jewish community today in pulpits, seminaries, journals, and books. However, it is to be admitted that with few exceptions there is little that is startlingly new about contemporary Jewish theology.[2] This lack of novelty does not mean a lack of interest or of brilliance. The ancient ideas are restated with vigor and beauty, but there is little of the frantic reaching for novelty which to an outsider at least seems to be so much a part of the theological scene within Christianity.

Nevertheless, it should be pointed out that contemporary Jewish theology and beliefs in practice have been conditioned by the two crucial events of modern Jewish life, the destruction of the Jews in Europe and the establishment of the independent Jewish state of Israel. These two events have formed the character of contemporary Jewish thought and must be taken into consideration in any discussion of what Jews, whether secular or religious, are thinking and doing.

The history of contemporary Judaism has also been greatly influenced by the emergence in this century of thinkers and writers whose thoughts have nurtured the religion, faith, and actions of contemporary Jews. Therefore, in order to understand what is going

---

1: Milton Himmelfarb, ed., *The Condition of Jewish Belief* (New York: Macmillan, 1966), pp. 4-5.
2. For a survey of current trends see Seymour Siegel, "The Current Theological Situation," *Conservative Judaism* 23 (Summer 1969): 11-24.

on in the theological world of contemporary Judaism, it is necessary briefly to discuss the impact on Judaism of four important thinkers: Martin Buber, Franz Rosenzweig, Abraham Heschel, and Mordecai Kaplan. Attention at least needs to be given to the salient points in their thought.

Since Martin Buber is the best known writer on Judaism in our time, it is not necessary here to analyze in depth the philosophical approach which has been identified with him. His is the epic-making teaching that there are two ways in which the world can be encountered by man. One is expressed in the primary word "I-Thou," and the other in the primary word "I-It." This insight has revolutionized philosophy, religion, psychology, sociology, politics and many other fields of human endeavor in this century.

In order to emphasize an important consideration of Buber in relationship to Judaism, it may be well to do what Buber always does—tell a story. This story, so far as is known, is not written anywhere. It happened when Professor Buber visited the United States for the first time in 1951 under the auspices of the Jewish Theological Seminary of America. During a seminar held at Columbia University to which many distinguished scholars and writers were invited to discuss with Buber problems raised by his thought, one of the questions put to Buber concerned a problem which at the time was being discussed at the United Nations. A participant asked him what he would do if he were a member of the United Nations. How would he vote in relationship to this issue? Buber answered that he could not tell in advance what he would do. He would enter with his whole being into the moment of decision and do what he was directed to do as he perceived it in the participation in the very moment of decision-making. Present at this seminar was Reinhold Niebuhr, who said to Buber, "The trouble with you, Professor Buber, is that you're too religious." Niebuhr's comment, as frequently was the case, was expressing a Jewish point of view in criticism of Buber.

Buber's radical existentialism tends to negate the existence of structures and principles which can be articulated before the fact, and his reliance upon the decision made within the context of the moment may put too much trust in the religious abilities of man. Buber's radical existentialism tends to negate the existence of organized religion since the structure of religion, as he expresses it, is an objectification of the primary encounter with, and the living response to, the eternal Thou, which is the heart of religion.

Therefore, Buber himself did not participate personally in the
ongoing, religious, organized life of the Jewish believing community.
This seems to be a flaw in his whole approach. Buber, in his classical
work *I and Thou*, said, "This is the exalted melancholy of our fate
that every Thou in our world must become an It."[3] Buber
recognized the fact, and spoke about it with a great deal of insight
and in a moving way, that I-Thou is not able to be sustained in real
life permanently, and that life in the real world requires also that
every Thou must become an It. Therefore, we have schools, voting
lists, telephone books, and contracts—all I-It manifestations by which
we order our life.

Buber was willing to grant that every Thou must become an It
with one exception, and that is in regard to religion. Here he insisted
that any religious form which is not in the category of I-Thou is
thereby illicit or at least non-religious, and this drew him away
personally from the organized, ongoing life of the Jewish believing
community.

For Buber, there is no fixed point in the sacred history (such as
Sinai): "The Jewish Bible does not set a past event as a mid-point
which cannot be pinned to any set time, . . . the mid-point in this
mortal and yet immortal moment of mine. . . . Revelation is not a
fixed, dated point. . . ."[4]

In Buber's philosophy of Judaism, the Jewish people are the
people covenanted to live on the dialogic plane with God and to
create true community. There are two main examples of true
community according to Buber. These were the Hasidic communities
of Eastern Europe in the early days of Hasidism, and the Kibbutzim
or communes in Israel today.

Buber's understanding of that great movement, Hasidism, focused
on the aspect which he believed stressed spontaneity and unmediated
encounter with God. Buber tended to overlook the fact, in his
account of Hasidism, that the Hasidim with all their fervor and with
all their spontaneity were, nevertheless, faithful adherents of Jewish
practice and observance.

It is curious that Christians often express surprise that the

---

3. Martin Buber, *I and Thou*, trans. Ronald Gregor Smith (New York: Charles Scribners
Sons, 1937), p. 16.
4. Martin Buber, "The Man of Today and the Jewish Bible," in *Israel and the World* (New
York: Schocken Books, 1948), p. 94.

Hasidim, who still exist in rather great numbers in this country and in Israel, are not proto-Christian sects who live off of grace, but instead are extremely meticulous in the observance of the minutae of Jewish mitzvot and commandments. However, it is the recovery of the hidden light of Hasidism which represents Buber's great contribution to Judaism.

Buber's attachment to Zionism from his earliest years focused on the creation of community within the Jewish commonwealth which would exemplify what would be to him the true aim of human life—an association of men attempting to live on the plane of I-Thou in true community. Buber's focus tended in many instances to alienate him from the Jewish masses because in his early days— although he changed later—he could not see the necessity for a Jewish state and advocated a bi-national state. It is important to recall the very moving words which Buber addressed to Mahatma Gandhi, the latter being critical of the Jewish rebirth and the attempts to resettle the ancient Holy Land. Buber said, "We need our own soil in order to fulfill it [our mission]; we need the freedom in order to order our life—no attempt can be made on foreign soil and under foreign statute. It cannot be that the soil and the freedom for fulfillment are denied us. We are not covetous, Mahatma; our one desire is that at last we may be able to obey."[5]

This emphasis on the establishment of a Jewish Commonwealth in Palestine and in Israel as an attempt finally to obey the covenant under conditions of independence and not of dependence, of majority status rather than minority status, is an extremely important contribution of Buberian thought to the Jewish consciousness today. However, it is important to remember that the emphases that Buber brought into the consciousness of the Jewish community tended to influence him and his followers away from the established pattern of Jewish life, which is defined by the poles of structure and spontaneity. His preference for spontaneity over structure and his denigration, therefore, of Jewish observance and Jewish liturgical practice tended to diminish Buber's influence on contemporary Judaism. For better or for worse, Jews are theoretically committed (they don't always put it in practice in their own life, of course) to the life of tradition and the Torah or the law, even when it is broadly

---

5. Martin Buber, "An Answer to Gandhi," in *Writings of Martin Buber*, ed. Will Herberg (Cleveland, Ohio: Meridian Books, 1956), p. 283.

defined as in liberal Judaism.

The great influence of Buber on the thought of contemporary Jews is in his emphasis on the encounter with God as being a real encounter of person to person in the midst of the world in which we live; this was his reaction to the depersonalized and rather anemic kind of liberal religion which nineteenth-century Judaism had created. It is not that we suffer from a lack of scientific application in our life, but that we have too much science; not that we are too much in the world of I-It, but that we are not in the world of I-Thou.

If a man were really to embrace the world, he would meet the living God with whom he could enter into encounter and dialogue. It is this recovery of the Biblical God and the Talmudic God, who is not an abstraction or a principle or an ideal, but a real reality which one meets in the midst of life as he responds to others and to the world, which has had an enormous impact upon the thinking of Jews and non-Jews as they contemplate their role within the Jewish community and their lives as men and women. This, of course, is especially true now as life has become so technological and bureaucratic.

More impactful on contemporary Judaism, but less well known, has been the thought of Buber's contemporary, Franz Rosenzweig, who unfortunately died at a young age and whose main work, *The Star of Redemption*,[6] has only this year just been translated into English. Rosenzweig's dramatic biography has stirred Jews almost as much as his thought. A brilliant young Jew who was born in 1886 in Germany, Rozenzweig was brought up in a liberal Jewish household in which his religious training was, to say the least, anemic.

At one time, he contemplated converting to Christianity. The pastor to whom he turned to arrange for his entrance into the Christian community told him that in order to become a Christian he would first have to become a Jew; in other words, to enter into the Christian covenant he should do so as the early Christians did. As the story goes, this incident happened just before the High Holidays. On the days of Rosh Hashana' and Yom Kippur, which are the most sacred days in the Jewish liturgical calendar, he chanced upon a traditional synagogue in Berlin. He was so moved by what happened there that, as he said, "I decided to remain a Jew."

---

6. Franz Rosenzweig, *The Star of Redemption*, trans. William W. Hallo (New York: Holt, Rinehart and Winston, 1971).

Rosenzweig wrote several books and collections of smaller writings and letters. His most influential book, *The Star of Redemption*, was written while he was serving in the German Army during the First World War on the Balkan front, which was fortunately very quiet; it made it possible for him to write his theology book on postal cards which he sent to his mother. His comrades wondered what kind of girl friend he had that he was writing such voluminous postal cards to her.

He called his philosophical stance the "New Thinking," which in academic language is called existentialist thinking, or another term which Rosenzweig used, "Life Thinking." This thinking involves making sense of existence and is a participant-thinking in life in contrast to a spectator type of thought; it is a thinking, as Rosenzweig said, in which man stakes his whole existence.

His religious orientation is signified by the title of his work, *The Star of Redemption*, which was built on the notion that the primary data of experience are three realities which cannot be reduced one to the other. These three realities are God, man, and the world. God is related to the world through creation and to man through revelation. Man is related to God also through revelation, and man after receiving the revelation of God turns to his fellow men with whom he tries to redeem the world so that it will resemble that which God intended it to be when He first created it. If you take God, man, and the world, and creation, revelation, and redemption, you will see that they are two triangles imposed one over the other which form the familiar Star of David which Rosenzweig called "The Star of Redemption."

Judaism, or rather Jewish life, is living within and through the Star of Redemption. Through attachment to the sacred year and to the sacred law, the believer is with the Father. Creation, revelation, and redemption are experienced through the observance of Judaism. The Jew living within the Star of Redemption experiences eternity and a relationship with the Father.

Rosenzweig's work has frequently been characterized as that of a third way between orthodoxy and liberalism, in relation to three crucial areas—the Bible, Jewish observance, and Christianity. In his view of the Bible, which he began to translate in collaboration with Buber, he eschews liberalism which sees the Bible merely as human inspiration and orthodoxy which sees it as a result of a kind of stenography or what Christians would call fundamentalism.

In a frequently quoted letter which Rosenzweig sent to a leader of German Jewry, he wrote that the Biblical material which the critics ascribe to the redactor who put everything together is for us *Rabenu,* our teacher. For it is through the redactor that those parts of the scripture which are necessary for our own illumination have been given to us. The traditions that are necessary for our illumination have been put together for us by the redactor who is our teacher or who has (and this is a pun) achieved a mosaic; i.e., the pieces when put together form the pattern of scriptures.

Rosenzweig is more popular than Buber in contemporary Judaism because in regard to Jewish observance he stressed the importance of Jewish Halakha (observance) as a way of living in the presence of God. He was not committed to Jewish liberalism, which in those days downgraded the importance of observance; nor did he embrace orthodoxy which says that every aspect of Jewish observance must be undertaken. But as a returner, as a *Baal Teshuva,* he said that a man should continue to include within his own life more and more observance as he is able to feel the power of religious living. When he was once asked whether he was completely observant, he answered, "Not yet." It is this "not yet" which breaches both liberalism which says "not at all," or orthodoxy which says "everything."

Most influential and best known is Rosenzweig's highly original theory about the relationship between Judaism and Christianity. Rosenzweig saw, as no other Jewish thinker before him, Christianity as important in salvation history. Rosenzweig did not share the belief of many Jewish thinkers that Christianity represents a version of Biblical religion which has abandoned the main beliefs of Judaism and is therefore to be reckoned as little more than a Jewish heresy. Nor did Rosenzweig accept the notion that all religions basically are the same, whether Jewish, Christian, Muslim, Hindu, and so forth (or as the Japanese say, all roads lead to Fujiyama), expressing eternal truth in their uniquely culturally influenced ways. This latter view, of course, is most characteristic of liberalism.

According to Rosenzweig there are two covenants which define the relationship between humankind and the divine. These two covenants are the covenant of Judaism and the covenant of Christianity. One is the covenant with the people of Israel in which the people of Israel establish their existence as God's people. Through the covenant of Israel the Jews are already with the Father, as Rosenzweig puts it, therefore Jewish recognition of Christianity rests, in fact, upon Christianity, namely on the fact that Christianity recognizes Judaism. It is the Torah, ultimately, which is spread abroad by Bible societies to the most distant islands. No one comes to the Father except through him, that is, Jesus. No one *comes*, but the situation is different when one need no longer come to the Father because he is already with him. That is the case of the nation of Israel.[7]

Christianity represents to Rosenzweig the Judaism of the Gentiles and represents a way in which the nations of the world establish their relationship with the Divine. In that case, the New Testament is new, not in the sense that it supercedes the "Old," but that it is newer or complementary to the "Old," providing a means by which the nations of the world come to the Father. So the Jewish people, who reside within the Star of Redemption, have already reached the Father.

Therefore, in a divine economy there is a division of labor. The Jewish people remain in history awaiting the final redemption in the presence of their Father and it is the Christian covenant which has been assigned the task of bringing the nations to God. Judaism is the sun, as Rosenzweig puts it, and Christianity constitutes the rays, and it is only at the end of time that both Christianity and Judaism will be united together.

This view of Rosenzweig gives Christianity a high value in God's view and it serves as a basis for a relationship between Judaism and Christianity in which each recognizes the integrity and the importance of the other. He had some very highly original things to say about the relationship between Judaism and Christianity. For example, he pointed out the absence of high liturgical art among the Jews and how impressed he was with Christian liturgical music and art. He explained this by referring to the fact that since the Jew was already born a Jew, he did not have to be converted to Judaism; whereas the Christian is born a pagan and must become a Christian, so that Christianity uses even the aesthetic sense to reach those who might not be reached any other way.

Rosenzweig had an interesting view of Christianity. He believed that Christianity was emerging into a new era, to the Johannine Era

---

7. Nahum Glatzer, *Franz Rosenzweig: His Life and Thought* (New York: Schocken Books, 1961), p. 341.

which was the era of the spirit, in contradistinction to the previous era, the Era of the Church. He thought something like Joachim of Fiore who taught that the Church had passed through the era of the Father, then the Son, and is soon to pass into the era of the Holy Spirit. Therefore Rosenzweig believed that Christianity also was going into a new phase wherein the relationships would be more benign.

Rosenzweig could say that the vocation of the Christian is to be part of the Christian community and to bring the nations of the world to the covenant. The inference of Rosenzweig's thought, with which many other Jews do not agree, is that it gives a very non-activist character to Judaism. Judaism (the Jewish people) is not to be active in history any more. Rosenzweig was not in favor of Zionism. Jews are already with the Father. They live in the Star of Redemption and partake in eternity and thereby have conquered death and wait until God fills up time as He no doubt will.

These three emphases of Rosenzweig—a view of the Bible which is serious but not fundamentalist, a view of Jewish observance which puts a higher value on the Jewish Halakha without insisting on a rigid orthodoxy, and the high evaluation of Christianity without sacrificing the integrity of Judaism—have made Rosenzweig an important part of the theological and religious consciousness of modern Judaism, especially that part of the Jewish people that lives in the West. The editor of *The Condition of Jewish Belief*,[8] Milton Himmelfarb, has enumerated the references to various thinkers in the thirty-eight essays published in that volume and found that Rosenzweig is the most widely quoted therein.

The third important influence on contemporary Jewish thought is Abraham Joshua Heschel, who is a Professor of Jewish Ethics and Mysticism at the Jewish Theological Seminary of America and, in contrast to Buber and Rosenzweig, has done most of his work here in the United States. He has published a number of very influential books on Jewish religion.

Heschel begins with the problem of how to know God. He asserts that there are three ways in which men can gain a perspective on the Divine. The first way is that of nature. Every sensitive person experiences what Heschel calls the sense of the ineffable, pointing to a Power or Being which is beyond and above nature. The glory of

---

8. Himmelfarb, *The Condition of Jewish Belief.*

God, the Hebrew word *Kavod*, represents the allusiveness of all things, pointing beyond themselves toward their Creator. The second way in which a man experiences a divine reality is through the revelation of God in the Bible and in the sacred writings based upon the Bible. We are brought face to face with this God when we sensitively read the Biblical literature. The Bible itself, according to Heschel, echoing the Rosenzweigian approach to scripture, is a great Midrash on the act of revelation, not to be identified with it, but in which the divine word has stimulated the human response.[9] The third way in which man is able to experience the divine is through the performance of what Heschel calls sacred deeds. Echoing a famous statement of the Middle Ages, Heschel says the way *to* God is the way *of* God. Rather than engage in a leap of faith, Heschel counsels that those who seek to deepen their religious life undertake a leap of action. In the doing of a sacred deed, another name for the Hebrew word *Mitzvah*, we are made to be aware of the reality which men call God.

Heschel has authored an eloquent defense of the Jewish system of observances and has given new life to the structure of Jewish *Halakha*. If we sensitively read the Bible and religiously perform the sacred deeds, what is the nature of the God that we find? Here Heschel has contributed a very important element in the understanding of the divine nature according to Biblical theology which is the basis of Judaism and Christianity. He calls this the discovery of the God of Pathos, that is to say, that the God of the prophets is not an unmoved mover. He is rather the most moved mover. God is affected by our failures and successes; prophecy is the religion of sympathy in which the prophet expresses God's anguish at men's misdeeds and his yearning for their return and repentance. God is, therefore, in need of man, in search of man, and consequently our relationship toward the divine should be a relationship of attempting to fulfill the divine demands made upon us. The essence of man is a sense of being needed, his being needed not only by other men but by the divine Himself.

God is characterized in the Biblical literature not so much by his perfection (which is a kind of Greek notion where God is completely

---

9. Abraham J. Heschel, *God in Search of Man* (Philadelphia: Jewish Publication Society, 1963), pp. 174-175, 168-173, 178-180, 184, 185, 187, 198-199.

self-sufficient, so to speak) but by his unity and uniqueness which are Hebraic emphases in which through him everything in reality is unified.

For Heschel, Judaism is the expression of God's needs and the response of man. Therefore, Jewish law is very important as a response to God's demands made upon us. In the light of these understandings, Heschel has written movingly about the inner meaning of Jewish observance, especially such important elements to Judaism as the Sabbath and the role of the land of Israel in Jewish consciousness. The powerfully written and evocatively phrased words of Heschel have affected the imagination of Jews and non-Jews and have brought them to a closer appreciation of the aspects of Judaism which have been associated with mysticism, Hasidism, and deep inner feeling. His expression and understanding of the nature of God as the God of Pathos, the God who suffers when men fail and who yearns for man's response to him, has been particularly influential in stressing both the role of the divine-human interplay in the redemption of history and the character of man who finds his essential meaning in response to the divine demand to perfect history and to make justice reign within the world.

A fourth thinker of great influence, Mordecai Kaplan, has many aspects of his thought in common with the other three theologians, but in many ways is crucially different. Kaplan is Professor Emeritus of Philosophy of Religion at the Jewish Theological Seminary. Educated in America, he brings into his thought and writings specifically American emphases. While his writings first appeared before World War II, Kaplan seems especially contemporary in analyzing the problems which confront Judaism in particular and traditional religion in general.

According to Kaplan, the problem of contemporary man is not the problem which Buber sees as living in a world of I-It. He believes the problem of contemporary man is that he inhabits a new universe of discourse, a universe which he believes is permeated through and through by natural law, by reliance on science for the validation of facts, and by the rejection of the supernatural element in life. He believes that traditional Judaism built on the notion of super-naturalism has to be reinterpreted.

He also notes the crisis in Jewish self-identity. Before modern times, Jews defined themselves as a religion within a hostile environment and had no trouble in understanding their essential character. With the growth of modern nationalism and its emphasis on secular identity in the larger national state, the status of Judaism has been questioned. Therefore, Kaplan has devoted a great deal of thought to the revaluation or the reconstruction (therefore his movement is called Reconstructionism) of traditional Judaism so that it can be restated in the light of modern nationalism and naturalism. It is his contention that we must reinterpret the idea of God not as a being among other beings nor as a power beyond nature who controls mundane life in history, but rather that we give the name God to those forces within the universe which make for salvation.

His famous utterance that "God is the power that makes for salvation"[10] has had a tremendous impact upon many contemporary Jews. God is to be understood as the sum total of those forces within the universe that are friendly to us and help us realize ourselves, our talents, and our hopes. He is to be understood, not as a being, but rather as a process and to be analyzed more by how he works than what he is. Wherever there are forces within life which lead men toward self-realization and the fulfillment of their dreams and aspirations, the divine is at work. There is indeed a close similarity to the thought of Henry Nelson Weiman in this.

In the light of the developments of modern nationalism, Kaplan asserts that Judaism is to be understood neither as a religion nor as a national entity, but as a civilization in which all the elements that define the civilization are included—religion, ethics, folkways, music, art, and other activities.

Jews in America live in two civilizations, a Jewish and an American civilization, and they should use both of them to enhance their lives as individuals and as Jews. Kaplan's call for a frank revaluation of Jewish theological concepts in the light of scientific advance and his efforts in redefining Jewish status in the light of modern naturalism and nationalism have been very impactful on the minds of contemporary Jews, both young and old.

In summarizing this very brief overview of the contributions of these four important theologians in contemporary Judaism, one can see them in relation to the three elements of Judaism: God, Israel, and Torah. Buber places the emphasis on the personalistic aspect of

---

10. Mordecai Kaplan, *The Greater Judaism in the Making: A Study in the Modern Evolution of Judaism* (New York: Reconstructionist Press, 1960), p. 470.

the divine-human encounter; on God's relationship to man, to history, and to the world. Heschel emphasizes God as needing man, and Kaplan, unlike the other three, stresses that God is helping us to achieve our salvation within the world. Buber, Heschel, and Rosenzweig affirm the chosenness of Israel and the importance of the land of Israel. Kaplan in his naturalistic term chooses to speak of the vocation of Israel and not the chosenness of Israel, but nonetheless stresses the importance of Zionism. With the exception of Buber, all stress the importance of Jewish observance as a way by which the Jew establishes his Jewishness, his humanity, and his relationship to God. All affirm the life of the Jewish people as a sacred entity.

As was observed at the beginning of this essay, the two events that have formed the character of modern Judaism have been the Nazi destruction of European Jews and the establishment in 1948 of the State of Israel.

On the matter of the Holocaust and its meaning, Buber was in Germany during the Nazi period and led the Jewish spiritual resistance to the Nazis. He wrote on the meaning of suffering; in an essay which is printed in his book *At The Turning*[11] he noted the meaning and the response which a contemporary Jew can give to the Holocaust. It was in this publication that he coined the expression "the eclipse of God," and in which he gave a highly original interpretation of the Book of Job. According to Buber's view, Job did not receive an answer to his question, which has of course been noted by many other writers and commentators. What the friends of Job said to him and what expressly added to his anguish was that there was no longer a dialogue between himself and God. The dialogue between heaven and earth had been cut off, and that is symbolized by Job's suffering and by the silence of God in the face of Job's complaints. At the end of the book of Job, God spoke to Job. God did not solve Job's problem, but he reestablished the dialogue between heaven and earth. Therefore, in the time of the eclipse of God, it is not that God is dead but that a cloud has passed; the believer should persist in his search for, and his turning toward, the eternal Thou.

---

11. Martin Buber, *At The Turning: Three Addresses on Judaism* (New York: Farrar, Straus and Young, 1952).

What is interesting about Kaplan, who tends to be so up-to-date, is that his book which was written in 1934 was republished in 1964 without any change at all. Although he is very concerned with the question of Zionism, he has not addressed himself to the question of the Holocaust.

Rosenzweig, of course, died in 1929. As for Heschel, although he has not written specifically about the Holocaust, it certainly permeates his writing.

The best conclusion to this brief study would be to hold two quotations in juxtaposition. One is by the French novelist, André Shwartz-Bart, who wrote the first great novel describing the meaning and pain of the Holocaust, *The Last of the Just.* At the end of *The Last of the Just* there is a poignant scene where Ernie, the hero, goes to the gas chamber together with his wife and a group of children. He says, "Oh Lord, we went forth like this thousands of years ago through the Red Sea of salt and bitter tears. Oh let us arrive soon."[12]

In an ecstatic article which appeared in the journal *Judaism* right after the Six-Day War, Professor Harold Fisch of Israel wrote, "The sea has split. We have walked through the Red Sea from the Egypt of Auschwitz to the coast of the Promised Land with the power of God holding the waters back at the right and at the left."[13] It is perhaps the juxtaposition of these two quotations that speaks most eloquently about the meaning and the direction of Jewish thought and determination today, and provides the context in which contemporary Jewish theology is to be received and understood.

---

12. André Schwartz-Bart, *The Last of the Just,* trans. Stephen Becker (London: Secker and Warburg, 1961).
13. Harold Fisch, "Jerusalem, Jerusalem," *Judaism* 16 (Summer 1967): 259-265.

PART THREE

CONTEMPORARY JEWISH-CHRISTIAN RELATIONS

IN ECUMENICAL PERSPECTIVE

Toward an Authentic Jewish–
Christian Relationship

A. Roy Eckardt

A true dialogic relation means that without surrendering his own integrity, a man apprehends another man in the other's self-understanding. Openness without self-identity violates the self; self-identity without openness violates the other. The self-identity out of which I speak is Christian, not Jewish or Jewish-Christian, yet it seeks to be open to the other, the Jew.

I

Insofar as the Christian faith takes history seriously, the confrontation between Jews and Christians in our time is conditioned, ineluctably, by two events and one threat: the European Holocaust and responsibility for it, the rebirth of the State of Israel, and the eventuality of a second Holocaust, namely, Israel's possible obliteration. Yet it is one thing to say that these events and this threat determine the confrontation between Jews and Christians, and it is something else to say—or to ask: Are these events and this threat of decisive meaning for the Christian as a Christian?

Dare we relate the Holocaust to the resurrection of the Jewish State? Certainly not in the way the Synod of the Hervormde Kerk (Reformed Church) of Holland recently implied. The Synod tells us that God's faithfulness is seen in the fact that "the Jewish people cannot be done away with."[1] With six million European Jews dead, three million Russian Jews under oppression, and the contingency of a new Holocaust in the Middle East, only false prophets promise that the Jews cannot die and that God will take care of them. (As he did

---

The present article is offered in dedication to Elie Wiesel.
1. The reference here is to a mimeographed English translation of a statement entitled *Israel: People, Land and State* recently adopted by the Synod of the Hervormde Kerk (Reformed Church) of Holland, paragraph 34.

in Auschwitz?) Yet is Abraham Heschel totally misguided in his work
Israel: An Echo of Eternity? He seems to fill the role of one of Elie
Wiesel's madmen, or perhaps of one who answers the madmen. Rabbi
Heschel testifies that "Israel enables us to bear the agony of
Auschwitz without radical despair, to sense a ray of God's radiance
in the jungles of history."[2]

The two events and the one threat lead us far away from a
peaceful academic discussion or a pleasant study group. The setting
that holds us is more of the nature of a *trial*. With a new Holocaust as
the threat of our time, President Douglas Young of the American
Institute of Holy Land Studies, Jerusalem, as much an academic man
as any of us, as well as a devout Christian, felt called to begin a
recent open letter to a fellow Christian with the words "I accuse." It
seems that the other man, editor of Canada's largest Christian
magazine, has been making a profession of antisemitism—defined,
strictly, as hostility to Jews—at the special expense of the people of
Israel. Dr. Young's words, "I accuse," are the ones that fit, not in an
emotional sense, but objectively. In the end he says, "I accuse you of
falling into bloody hands and allowing your own to become stained
with that blood. . . ."[3] There is a trial under way, and much of our
existential dilemma is to try to learn which role is ours: Judge?
Defendant? Plaintiff? Jury? Witness? Onlooker? Who am I?

II

Among the major defendants at the trial is God himself. I do not
think that the questions, Is God dead? Is he not dead?, are the real
ones. The excruciating question is whether, if God lives and is not
helpless, he ought to go on living, he who has permitted the death of
the six million. For an embittered Jakov Lind, in the Holocaust are
"the flames of God's ever-burning love for his chosen people." The
issue is not so much whether God can live in a human presence as it
is whether he can live with himself. For even after Auschwitz, God
does not seem to be exactly working hard to prevent a recurrence
(not to mention the fate of all kinds of other people: the American
Blacks, the Indians, and on and on). Must not the words be flung at

---

2. Abraham Joshua Heschel, *Israel: An Echo of Eternity* (New York: Farrar, Straus and
Giroux, 1969), p. 115.
3. From an open letter by Douglas Young to A. C. Forrest, 1 August 1969.

him as well: "I accuse"? I am only your little child, and not a very good one. But what kind of a Father are you, God?

From an opposite vantage point, Emil L. Fackenheim asks: "Has [Hitler] succeeded in destroying the Jewish faith for us who have escaped?"[4] Of course, I have not escaped from anything. I am *a survivor of nothing*, really. But there are survivors. In behalf of them Zvi Kolitz, co-producer of Rolf Hochhuth's drama, *Der Stellvertreter (The Representative)*, reconstructs the last thoughts of a pious Jew, Yossel Rakover. We have no actual document from Rakover. But we know that a Yossel Rakover did die in the flames. Kolitz has him addressing God in this wise:

You may insult me, you may castigate me, you may take from me all that I cherish and hold dear in the world, you may torture me to death—I shall believe in *you*, I shall love you no matter what you do to test me.

And these are my last words to you, my wrathful God: nothing will avail you in the least. You have done everything to make me renounce you, to make me lose my faith in you, but I die exactly as I have lived, a *believer!*

Eternally praised be the God of the dead, the God of vengeance, of truth and of law, who will soon show his face to the world again, and shake its foundations with his almighty voice.

Hear, O Israel, the Lord our God the Lord is One.

Into your hands, O Lord, I consign my soul.[5]

These are the choices for Jews: the abandonment of God; the post-Auschwitz affirmation of God. Even the second alternative reflects, with the first, a degree of contumaciousness toward God, dead or alive—on the unassailable basis that in such an event as the Holocaust the Jew is the victim. The alternatives for the Christian are different—because Christians (and I do not speak of them indiscriminately) have been among the executioners and the friends of executioners. Accordingly, the Christian's temptation is not so much contempt for God as contempt for himself (in contrast to self-acceptance). The question for me as a Christian is not so much "Does God live?" as it is "Do I still live, or have I destroyed myself?" Have we who are Christians despoiled our integrity? The prime question to Jews is suffering; the prime question to Christians is guilt.

---

4. Emil Fackenheim, *God's Presence in History: Jewish Affirmations and Theological Reflections* (New York: New York University Press, 1970), p. 71.
5. Zvi Kolitz, "Yossel Rakover's Appeal to God," *Trends: A Journal of Resources* 1 (February 1969): 32.

III

It is already manifest that two sorts of issues face us: the objective theological question of God's will, his righteousness—the question of truth—and the existential question of human moral responsibility and culpability. We have to grapple with both issues if we are to approximate an authentic Jewish-Christian relationship for our time.

Constructively, we may begin with a problem that Christians have but that Jews do not have, at least not to the same degree. From the Jewish side, to be a human being is to be a Jew, and to be a Jew is to be a human being. There is no separation between the two elements. In the Halachic tradition, a Jew is someone born of a Jewish mother. For the male child, circumcision is the symbolic acknowledgment and celebration of Jewishness; it does not create Jewishness. But in the Christian tradition, we would be incorrect to assert that a Christian is someone born of a Christian mother—or father, for that matter. If one is a Jew simply by being born, to be a Christian (by contrast), one must *do* something: he must make a decision, a decision of faith. Jewishness means peopleness. But Christianity is a religion. Without entering into the possible conflict between infant baptism and adult baptism, one has to say that in the Christian view, baptism represents a fundamental decision. The gentile child, for example, may say "no" to his parents' desire that he be a Christian—and then he is not a Christian. The child of Jewish parents may say "no" to his family's religious wishes for him, but this does not make him any less a Jew. He may be a poor Jew, from his parents' standpoint, but he is still a Jew.

One may inquire what all this has to do with the problem I said Christians have. It has everything to do with it. For me to accept the Christian faith is, for me, to be granted answers to questions that confront me as a human being. But when the Jew affirms the Jewish faith, he receives answers to questions that confront him as someone who is already a Jew. And there is all the difference in the world between these two states of affairs. A Jew can be an atheist without ceasing to be a Jew. But the idea of a Christian atheist remains a contradiction in terms.

IV

Let us take a further step. The question to the Christian is how he might be accepted by God. Here the difference between us is enormous. The question of how the Jew may be accepted by God as an individual human being is not a life-and-death matter for the Jew. What counts is participation in Jewish peopleness. And the Jewish people are, as Franz Rosenzweig would express it, already with God—at least once the stance of Yossel Rakover is taken. The Jews are already part of the community of God's people, participants in an age-old covenant. As Jews, they do not have to "be saved" (as against what Christians say); Jews are already the children of Abraham, Isaac, and Jacob. By being children of the fathers—the patriarchs—they are children of their heavenly Father. The covenant with Abraham and his people is an abiding covenant.

The claim of an elect nation of Israel is a most delicate one. Later I will raise questions about it. For the moment I only ask that my present intention be kept in mind: to point up the nature of the Christian's problem. In that context I worry not so much about possible offense among Jews when the conviction of Jewish chosenness is expressed by, of all people, a Christian, as I worry over something else: If it is so that the Lord has pledged his faithfulness to Israel, the question is: How may his abiding covenant be extended to us who are poor pagans?

Christians believe, or they hope (faith and hope are very close)—Christians *trust* that through the grace of God in Jesus the Jew, they are made fellow members with Israel in the covenant. The covenant is, so to say, opened upon the world. The writer of the letter to the Ephesians reminds his readers that before Christ came, they were, as gentiles, strangers to "the commonwealth of Israel," outside "the covenants of promise, having no hope and without God in the world." Yet through the grace that burst forth in Jesus they "are no longer strangers and sojourners, but . . . fellow citizens with the saints and members of the household of God, built upon the foundation of the apostles and prophets, Christ Jesus himself being the chief cornerstone. . . . (Eph. 2:11-20).

Genuine dialogue is unwavering in its honesty. The Christian is the man who dares to hope that he belongs in some all-decisive way to the family of Jews—even when he knows that such testimony may very well have to be rejected by that family. A parallel here is that Jews testify, to Christians, that the Christ, the Messiah, has not come—even when they know that such a denial is against the deep persuasion of the Christians they face.

V

Having brought in the messianic question—the importunate question across the centuries—let me reaffirm, with a number of convincedly Christian colleagues, opposition to any avowed effort on the part of the church to missionize the Jewish community as such. I do this not on moral grounds, although there are moral consequences here, but on strictly Christian confessional-theological grounds. For if the Jewish people are not already amongst the family of God, we who are gentiles remain lost and without hope. The covenant into which Jesus of Nazareth ostensibly leads us would be revealed as an illusion. By seeking to do away with the Jewish community as an indissoluble union of faith and people, the missionary position is, in truth, a veiled and perhaps below-conscious attack upon the integrity of the Christian faith—through assaulting the very foundation of Christianity: the Jewish people and their covenant with the Living God.[6]

Frank Cross, Jr., the Protestant New Testament analyst, applies the Pauline teaching in Romans 11 to the sphere of Jewish-Christian relations in this way: The church "affirms the validity and eternity" of the election and vocation of Israel. Christians are never permitted to "refer to Judaism as 'another religion,' or as a false form of the biblical faith." It is into the eternal covenant with Israel that Christians are grafted, as a wild olive branch is grafted into the root of a domestic olive tree. "The two covenants are one covenant just as the eternal covenant of Israel is identical with the new or rather renewed covenant" of the church.[7]

The Jewish community cannot accept as Messiah and Lord, Jesus of Nazareth. The point of view of the Jewish people is represented movingly by Martin Buber, of blessed memory: "Standing bound and shackled in the pillory of mankind, we demonstrate with the bloody body of our people the unredeemedness of the world."[8] The Jew experiences most intensely "the world's lack of redemption. He feels [it] against his skin, he tastes it on his tongue, the burden of the

---

6. A. Roy Eckardt, *Elder and Younger Brothers: The Encounter of Jews and Christians* (New York: Charles Scribner's Sons, 1967), pp. 157-158.
7. Frank M. Cross, Jr., "A Christian Understanding of the Election of Israel," *Andover Newton Quarterly* 8 (March 1968): 237, 240.
8. Martin Buber, *Ereignisse und Begegnungen* (Leipzig: Insel-Verlag, 1920), p. 20.

unredeemed world lies on him." Because of this knowledge "he *cannot* concede that the redemption has taken place; he knows that it has not."[9] This is why we must understand, as Christians, that the Jewish non-acceptance of Jesus as the Christ is an act of faithfulness to the God of the covenant, and *not,* as in the historic Christian polemic, an act of faithlessness.

Dr. Buber, with characteristic charity, goes on to speak on behalf of the Christian side. He writes that the Christian is the "daring man" who insists that "the redemption of the world has been accomplished."[10] With this judgment we may at once agree and disagree. At best, the redemption that Christians find in Jesus is only a start. The uniqueness of Christianity is its faith in the resurrection of Jesus. The Christian religion affirms the victory of God over nature, through his victory over death. Yet, at best, Jesus is only, in Saint Paul's words, the "first fruits of the harvest of those who have died" (I Cor. 15:20). Death is still a stern reality—and so are human prejudice and war and disease and loneliness. The Christian can only hope for the final redemption. In this, he joins his Jewish brothers, who, as they rejoice in and obey the precepts of Torah, also live in expectation of the Messianic Kingdom.[11] At the Seder, the cup of wine is set out for Elijah, herald of the Messiah. So, too, in the Christian communion ritual, the words attributed to Jesus are repeated, "I tell you I shall not drink again of the fruit of the vine until that day when I drink it new with you in my Father's kingdom" (Mark 14:25). The Jew and the Christian are men of tomorrow—these foolish, blessed men of hope, these children who dream impossible dreams.

VI

Having affirmed a covenantal theology, I must now share with you some of my misgivings, or at least questionings.

I have elsewhere suggested that Christian intervention in the doctrine of Israel's election easily opens the way to immorality. For the Christian, things come to a terrible impasse: We must speak of God—because we claim to be members of his family, if only by

---

9. Martin Buber, *Israel and the World* (New York: Schocken Books, 1948), p. 35.
10. Ibid., p. 40.
11. Eckardt, *Elder and Younger Brothers*, p. 160.

adoption. Yet we have despoiled his household. The covenant is broken—not by the Jews, not by the Lord—but it is broken. We Christians have broken it. Jewish suffering is Christian guilt. And so much of the guilt remains unappropriated. We would feel our guilt more if we *knew* more. At this point, I think the educationists are right. If only we Christians knew our Christian history, knew it in the sense of appropriating it into our own existence. I refer, of course, to 1600 years of Christian denigration and persecution of Jews and their faith. Ignorance is a drug that deadens the pain of guilt, and thereby deprives us of any effective catharsis.

A Beggar in Jerusalem says that at Sinai, God gave Israel the Torah, and in "the kingdom of night," the Holocaust, he took it back again.[12] Why should God do that? Because we heathen brought him so much grief. Therefore, this is the age after the covenant, this is the post-covenant time. Prophecy has ceased, revelation has stopped, the Torah is in a sense gone. Perhaps all that is left is for the Jewish people to tell tales. It may be that we Christians cannot do that. For us to tell the tale is only to speak of our shame. Perhaps all that we have left is the tale of a meeting, between those who have survived and us who have survived nothing.

How, then, are we to speak of the covenant? How, then, are we to speak of election? How, then, are we to speak of the God of Israel? Near the beginning I alluded to an issue that is joined in current Jewish thinking: On the one side, there is the negation of God *because* of the Holocaust. Richard L. Rubenstein, for example, views the God of "the kingdom of night" as a "cosmic sadist" who is beneath our contempt, or at least unworthy of our worship. On the other side, there is the affirmation of God *despite* the Holocaust, as in Emil L. Fackenheim. What is the Christian theologian to say?

If history can never demonstrate faith, neither can history (including the most horrible evils) ever disprove faith. *Theologically*, therefore, the Christian sides with Professor Fackenheim, the believer. Yet, *dialogically*, the Christian does not contradict Rabbi Rubenstein, the nonbeliever. For while Christian atheism is out of the question, Jewish atheism is not. And because of the peculiar relation between Christians and Jews—specifically, Christian com-

---

12. Elie Wiesel, *A Beggar in Jerusalem* (New York: Random House, 1970), p. 200; Samuel H. Dresner, "The Elie Wiesel Phenomenon: 2. Witness for Judaism," *Conservative Judaism* 25 (Fall 1970): 36.

plicity in the genocide and harassment of the Jewish people—there is one place where the Christian travels the road with Rubenstein. In this time after the covenant, Christians are forbidden to speak of Jewish election in the traditional sense—yet for an entirely different reason from the arrogant judgment in the churches that Jewish election is annulled by the inauguration of the "new Israel."

The reason we are now forbidden to speak of Jewish election is that there is no way to immunize the traditional, historic testimony to that election against satanic culpability for the incredible suffering of Jews. At the Holocaust the covenant went up in flames. God took back the Torah.

This reasoning does not have to conflict with Emil L. Fackenheim's assertion that it is blasphemous to find any positive purpose or justification in Auschwitz. Such reasoning is further consistent with Fackenheim's plea that Adolf Hitler not be granted a posthumous victory. For if the doctrine of Jewish election is to be retained in some form, this can only be done through its detheologization, its total moralization and total secularization, that is to say, through the avowal of election-beyond-suffering, of election-to-live, of Jewish normality. We are left with the 614th commandment: the command to survive. Professor Fackenheim asks: "Is not, after Auschwitz, any Jewish willingness to suffer martyrdom, instead of an inspiration to potential saints, much rather an encouragement to potential criminals? After Auschwitz, is not even the saintliest Jew driven to the inexorable conclusion that he owes the moral obligation to the antisemites of the world not to encourage them by his own powerlessness?"[13] Martyrdom was once a Jewish way of sanctifying the name of God. I believe that this is no longer possible.

We may celebrate the resurrection of Israel yet *never* justify the crucifixion of Auschwitz as *any* kind of exchange for Israel. Even to think of such justification is to gaze into the abyss of Evil. The way of reasoning proposed here is vindicated, I am emboldened to say, in and through a contemporary caveat: While the eye of faith may discern an ultimate correlation of Auschwitz-Israel—Israel as a "ray of God's radiance in the jungles of history"—this correlation can *never* be applied to the historical-political domain without playing into the hands of those who demand the annihilation of Israel on

---

13. Fackenheim, *God's Presence in History*, pp. 75-76.

such a moral ground as that many non-Jews have been made to suffer for the sins of other non-Jews. In contrast to the correlation argument we may attest, with James Parkes, that "the moral right of Jewry to an autonomous community in the Land of Israel has nothing to do with atonement for Europe or with the survival of Auschwitz. It rests on solid historical evidence—the continuous presence of a Jewish community from Masada to Balfour, and its place in Jewish history."[14] Had there been no Auschwitz, the right of the Jewish people to Israel would not be one wit lessened—any more than would the rights of other Palestinians.

In some such way as the foregoing we may begin, perhaps, to represent Professor Fackenheim as protagonist before Rabbi Rubenstein, and Rubenstein as protagonist before Fackenheim, as meanwhile we represent another Jewish protagonist, Jesus of Nazareth, who suffered before his Resurrection but does not suffer after it.

VII

It was proposed at the outset that the State of Israel determines the nature of today's confrontation of Jews and Christians as much as does the Holocaust. The major secular-moral lesson of Israel is that *the eternal minority is no longer a minority.* Again, I quote Richard Rubenstein: The State of Israel means "the massive refusal of the survivors of Auschwitz ever again to live as a part of Christian Europe." These survivors resolved, in effect: "We may die on the sands of Palestine, but we will never again accommodate ourselves to your good graces or your prejudices. There may some day be another Masada. . . . There will never be another Auschwitz."[15]

Is the same to be said for the American scene as for Christian Europe? In principle, here as well the minority days are gone. Because of Israel, the Jews among us are spiritually free—for now, at least. True, Jews who are *forced* to remain beyond Eretz Yisrael live in unrelieved exile. They are in captivity. But of those who can freely choose, and who choose to pass their days in a land other than Israel,

---

14. James Parkes, review of Alan T. Davies, *Anti-Semitism and the Christian Mind* in *Jewish Chronicle* (London), 3 April 1970.
15. Richard L. Rubenstein, Foreword to Alan T. Davies, *Anti-Semitism and the Christian Mind: The Crisis of Conscience After Auschwitz* (New York: Herder and Herder, 1969), p. 11.

the Diaspora gains authenticity. It is the State of Israel that makes the choice possible. Without Israel, there is no such freedom, and every Jew is held in exile. With Israel, the Jew of the Diaspora is sustained in every moment. He knows that he can be welcomed home—unconditionally. He is free—not to return or to return.[16]

Is there, then, nothing of exile in free Diaspora life? Unhappily, no. Israel herself is not spared the threat of obliteration. Nevertheless, she grants Jews courage to be responsible men *despite* the reign of the devilish powers. Are only Jews given courage? I wonder. David Polish writes, "The capacity of a people to face the demonic in man and to overwhelm its own fate is a vindication not only of this people, Israel, but of the spirit of man. . . ." Because of Israel, Jews in the Diaspora-exile may stand tall—and so may every man.[17]

Yes, Israel changes the whole nature of the erstwhile Jewish-Christian relationship. We Christians are finally defeated, and this is very good for us. We are defeated by the sovereignty of one tiny land. The Jewish-Christian confrontation of almost two millennia is totally transformed.

VIII

Since I speak as a Christian, perhaps my final word here can permissibly be a uniquely Christian testimony. If the State of Israel is a Jewish declaration of independence from the Christian world, the Christian from his side cannot consent to the breaking of the tie. Here the Christian is stiff-necked! He is only an adopted son, true, and a prodigal at that. Yet he is not prepared to be put out of the house. Buber assures us Christians that we are the "daring men." We may even dare to call upon the name of the Jew Jesus of Nazareth to intercede for us against banishment. Will not this Jewish man help us to live and to die with other Jewish brothers?

An American church official recently said that for Jews the future of the State of Israel "is the future of their people, but I'm not part of that people. . . ." This churchman was not right, I think. We who are Christians *are* part of the Jewish people—by the very nature of

---

16. Alice and Roy Eckardt, *Encounter With Israel: A Challenge to Conscience* (New York: Association Press, 1970), p. 252.
17. David Polish, "The Tasks of Israel and Galut," *Judaism* 28 (Winter 1969): 15; Eckardt and Eckardt, *Encounter With Israel*, pp. 252-253.

our Christian faith. We claim membership in the Jewish family. Therefore, Israel grasps us in our very existence, not merely as human beings (as men, we will simply try to be humanitarian); Israel grasps us as Christians. By virtue of our Christian existence, Israel can never be just another country. Of course, to the extent that it is on its own, Christianity is devoid of spatial ties. "But through its indissoluble bond with the Jewish people and the Jewish faith, the Christian faith is yoked spiritually to Eretz Yisrael."[18]

Perhaps all that needs to be added is that this same Christian bond with Jews extends to every dimension of the Jewish-Christian relationship. David Demson of Emanuel College, Toronto, has observed that the Christian "does not merely notice Jewish existence (as a sign of God's promise), but is committed to be a *defender* of Jewish existence. The Christian is committed to the defense of the Jew, just as a brother is committed to defense of brother in the house of their father. . . . If . . . the Christian repels the Jew from the house, the Christian will do well to remember that he is also repelling the will of the Lord, who has invited both Jew and Christian into his house."[19]

18. Eckardt and Eckardt, *Encounter With Israel*, p. 262.
19. David Demson, "Christians and Israel," *The Ecumenist* 7 (November-December 1968): 14.

Studies in the Interrelationships between America and the Holy Land: A Fruitful Field for Interdisciplinary and Interfaith Cooperation

ROBERT T. HANDY

I. METHOD

Some twenty years ago as I was developing courses and research projects in American religious history, I faced the problem of how I as a Christian church historian could deal fairly and perceptively with American Jewish history. How was a teacher in a Christian theological seminary to deal with Jewish life honestly and sensitively, especially when the whole complex world of Jewish studies was little known to me?[1] A few forays into the field showed how vast the area of ignorance was—the terms being used, the bibliographies, the authorities were largely unknown. Then an opportunity came to spend some time working in the field of the historical interrelationships between America and the Holy Land. This approach allowed me to move from topics in the history of Christianity about which I had some acquaintance towards what were for me new horizons. For the Holy Land has from the earliest days of European settlement on this continent had a special appeal and fascination for many kinds of people. To try to understand the complex attitudes that Christians in America have held and do hold towards the land in which our faith was born was a good place for me to start, beginning with materials about which I had some knowledge. But the Holy Land has a degree of holiness for Jews that is different from what it means for Christians, and the study of America-Holy Land interrelationships draws the scholar to try to understand as fully as he can what its special meaning is and why it is. This approach provides one way for the non-Jewish teacher to interpret Jewish life and history from a point of reference basic to it rather than from an external point.

---

1. A general article that gives some sense of the vastness and complexity of the field of Jewish studies is by Jacob Neusner, "Graduate Education in Judaica: Problems and Prospects," *Journal of the American Academy of Religion* 37 (1969): 321-330.

Both Christianity and Judaism in America are highly pluralistic phenomena with complex inner divisions. Attitudes concerning the Holy Land have often varied greatly within the many groupings and subgroupings of the two faiths. Though one may wish to focus primarily on the spiritual and theological significance of the Holy Land for the people of faith, still there have always been political aspects and overtones related to the Holy Land that cannot be simply screened out. To probe into human behavior at any real depth is always difficult; to probe into it when both religious and political emotions are so deeply involved is doubly so. Confronted with groups which hold differing religious and political attitudes toward Palestine and Israel, the inquirer is well advised to adopt some scholarly discipline and use it wisely and consistently if he is to move to significantly deeper understandings.

As a church historian, the historical method was of course the one I was best prepared to use in attempting to deal with interrelationships between America and the Holy Land in the nineteenth and twentieth centuries. A scholarly discipline is a useful instrument, a viable tool if used consistently and with integrity, but not an absolute in itself. Historical method cannot give us any ultimate objectivity or eliminate the subjectivities that are an inescapable part of human life. Faithfully used, the method can drive us to recognize our own premises and provincialisms; it can help us to keep them under review and under consideration—often a painful process, by the way. It can also provide us a way to work creatively with others of quite different backgrounds and presuppositions. For historical method demands that we get back to the sources and use them honestly and critically, even when they run counter to positions and commitments we may hold. Historical method insists that we back our generalizations with evidence, and submit both our interpretations and the sources on which they rest to those who differ from us, even to those whose views are diametrically opposed to our own.

The techniques of critical historical research, like those of other disciplines, can be employed by people of varying backgrounds and religions. Some faiths do incline many of their followers to take scholarship seriously. With a host of other Christians through the centuries I find my own commitment to the Christian way supports and undergirds my efforts to use scholarly disciplines seriously. Christian faith asserts that the world and mankind are God's creation, and hence the discovery and clarification of truths about creation and the creatures can lead to certain kinds of deeper understandings of the Creator. The faith is aware of the sinfulness and self-centeredness of man; scholarly disciplines can help to keep us honest and to guard against our own tendencies to slant the evidence to support our own particular views. Hence when this church historian undertook to do a little study in the intriguing but difficult field of the historical relationships between America and the Holy Land, he resolved to approach all matters in the tradition of the critical search for truth, and as a Christian seeker. Very soon I found that Jewish faith enjoins many of its followers to fruitful use of scholarly instruments (and at the same time, of course, to get interest in the Holy Land), and some fruitful partnerships and a joint seminar on America and the Holy Land have developed.[2]

The Christian scholar who seeks to work in an area that draws him into close study of topics relating to Judaism and in close cooperation with Jewish scholars may find he has certain inner and outer resistances to overcome, that is, resistances within himself and among others of his faith. In working at such a topic as the America-Holy Land relationship (and the same would be true for many other topics), the long, unhappy story of the Christian-Jewish tragedy is never very far from the surface. That the Christian churches throughout the centuries have treated Jews in prejudiced and unjust ways is written so plain on the record that no honest look at the evidence can deny it. When one is deeply devoted to the Christian way, and has found salvation and meaning for life in that faith, it is painful to have to look at the shortcomings. The story of Christian anti-Semitism began early; its traces can be found in the New Testament writings, in the Fathers of the Church, and in the Reformers. Though happily we live in a day when much of the anti-Semitism of the past has been repudiated by many in the churches, still the blight has by no means disappeared, and even in the most repentant circles of church life the shadows of prejudice are

---

2. The seminar, jointly sponsored by Union Theological Seminary and The Jewish Theological Seminary of America, has been conducted twice with the cooperation of Dr. Moshe Davis, Stephen S. Wise Professor of American Jewish History and Institutions, The Hebrew University of Jerusalem, and Research Professor of American Jewish History at Jewish Theological Seminary. With Dr. Selig Adler, Samuel P. Capen Professor of American History at the State University of New York at Buffalo, and others, we are seeking to gather and publish basic documentary materials for the continuing study of America and the Holy Land.

not yet wholly dispelled. The monstrous evil of the slaughter of European Jewry under Hitler was anti-Christian as well as anti-Semitic, yet it was carried out by many who were among the baptized, and grew on grounds prepared in part by Christian anti-Semitism. The mind and the spirit shrink from facing up to the terrible evil of the Holocaust; it takes considerable determination to get involved with a field that requires attention to that unhappy period.

Furthermore, the story of America and the Holy Land, when brought up to date, carries one into the turmoil of an intense political polarization, that of the Arab-Israeli struggle in the Middle East. Like most such arenas of intense controversy, this one is filled with complex disagreements. On both sides are sincere partisans who are deeply versed in the background and the details of the struggle, and who leap to fill you in on what to them is the right view of the matter. There are so many considerations on both sides—how can the seeker know how he should come down on the tangled issues? There are the deep religious devotion of Jewish residence and settlement in Palestine, the Balfour declaration of 1917 and the United Nations resolution, and the obvious need for a Jewish refuge and a homeland; there are also the facts of the dispossession of Arabs, the continuing and deteriorating Arab refugee problems, the presence of Arab Christian communities, the reactions of the so-called "new left" to Zionism, to list only a few of the particulars. It is difficult for one not directly involved to decide where he stands in matters of such intense controversy. Hence the Christian scholar may have to overcome some inner and outer resistances before moving into an area that involves him in such complexities and controversies. There are other, more theological reasons why this is a difficult business, such as the interpretation of the person and work of Jesus Christ, and the way a missionary religion like Christianity should confront the faithful of other religions.

Difficult problems do not go away by being ignored, however; they may even get worse. In my view, scholarship is a disciplined way to get at problems of intense personal and social concern. The Christian scholar can only hope that his efforts to understand and to clarify may in some way contribute to the discovery of truth, the overcoming of injustice, the elimination of prejudice, the reconciliation of polarities and the increase of love among men. Since getting involved a little in the historical study of America and the Holy

Land, and working with Jewish scholars in the effort, I have come to have a much deeper and better informed understanding and appreciation of Jews and of Judaism than I had, before. There are many avenues toward human understanding and reconciliation; this way of cooperative scholarship is only one. But for me it has been a great way; in working together with others in research and teaching the deeper meaning of historic faiths as they show up in daily attitudes and behavior has been brought home to me in vivid ways. What may have been abstractions about another religion suddenly become embodied in persons. Closeness with others of a different tradition can also increase perception of the depths in one's own faith, for he can look at himself in part through the eyes of the other. The effort to explain one's religious tradition to another can contribute to one's own grasp of it. Whenever Christians seek to explain themselves to others we can and should speak of the meaning of God, Christ, the Spirit, and the Church. When Jews seek to explain themselves to us they can and should speak of God, Torah, and Israel.[3] As Monsignor John M. Oesterreicher has put it, "To the religious Jew, God, Torah, and Israel, that is, the people and its land, are one; to the Christian, they are on quite different planes."[4] By perceiving those differences in depth we can come to a deeper human and religious understanding, if we only take one another seriously. The distinguished Jewish scholar David Flusser has remarked, "I think that out of an authentic feeling of fraternity for our Christian brethren, we are obliged to take seriously their ecclesiastical interpretation of the Old Testament. . . ."[5] So out of an authentic feeling of fraternity for Jewish brethren, we must take seriously their understanding of the land of Israel and its deep meaning for them. Participation in rigorous scholarly effort is precisely a way to take one another seriously.

---

3. E.g., see the chapter by Abraham J. Heschel, "God, Torah, and Israel," in Edward LeRoy Long, Jr. and Robert T. Handy, eds., *Theology and Church in Times of Change* (Philadelphia: Westminster Press, 1970), pp. 71-90.
4. John M. Oesterreicher, "The Theologian and the Land of Israel," *The Bridge, Judaeo-Christian Studies*, vol. 5, *Brothers in Hope*, ed. John M. Oesterreicher (New York: Herder and Herder, 1970), p. 239.
5. David Flusser, "The Jews—'a problem for the other,' " *The Jerusalem Post*, 20 November 1970.

II. America and Zion

The study of the historical relationships between America and the Holy Land is a complex one with many facets. It can be approached from many angles. Yet the field is sufficiently delimited, dealing with two countries over some three and a half centuries, that it can be ploughed with scholarly profit. There are, however, many strands to be followed in the effort to weave a broad tapestry of understanding. Characteristically, Jewish and Christian students will be drawn to different topics, for it is logical for one to begin in an area that he has at least partially explored. The Christian, who is seeking to understand at a deeper level the basis for historic attitudes in the Church to Judaism, may find it especially useful to explore how such concepts as the Promised Land, Zion, the Chosen People, and the Holy City have been used in Christian life. Generation after generation of American Christians have taken certain Biblical images relating to the Holy Land and transferred them from Palestine to America. In discussing the place of the Bible in American fiction, Carlos Baker remarked that

Again and again in the history of American letters we find writers using metaphors of Biblical origin. Not least among these is the great synoptic metaphor which so stimulated the imaginations of the American colonists in the seventeenth and eighteenth centuries that they thought and spoke of themselves under the image of the Chosen People, undertaking a task of plantation as the crowning act in God's providential plan. Not only did they call America the Promised Land, but also, as Perry Miller has observed, "they grew to regard themselves as so like the Jews that every anecdote of tribal history seemed like a part of their own recollection."[6]

The transferral of Holy Land imagery with all its richness to the new world has been characteristic of many types of American Christians. Much of the difficulty that Christians have had in understanding their Jewish brethren has arisen because those who have made the transfer quite completely may have trouble understanding those who have made such a shift only in part or not at all.

The annals of Christianity in America are full of illustrations of

---

6. Carlos Baker, "The Place of the Bible in American Fiction," in *Religion in American Life*, vol. 2, *Religious Perspectives in American Culture*, ed. James Ward Smith and A. Leland Jamison (Princeton, N.J.: Princeton University Press, 1961), p. 245.

the transfer of Zion, and of the spiritualizing of the Zion idea.[7] It has rarely been summed up more precisely than by Charles Hodge, that staunch nineteenth-century defender of Old-School Calvinist theology, in his massive and influential *Systematic Theology*. He wrote,

> It is undeniable that the ancient prophets in predicting the events of the Messianic period and the future of Christ's kingdom, borrowed their language and imagery from the Old Testament institutions and usages. The Messiah is often called David; his church is called Jerusalem, and Zion; his people are called Israel; Canaan was the land of their inheritance; the loss of God's favour was expressed by saying that they had forfeited that inheritance, and restoration to his favour was denoted by a return to the promised land. This usage is so pervading that the conviction produced by it on the minds of Christians is indelible. To them, Zion and Jerusalem are the Church and not the city made with hands. To interpret all that the ancient prophets say of Jerusalem of an earthly city, and all that is said of Israel to the Jewish nation, would be to bring down heaven to earth, . . .[8]

The "indelible" conviction on the mind of Christians was further accented by the usage of Promised Land and Zion imagery in hymns, spirituals, and popular religious literature. Zion imagery has long been used in Christian history to support the concept of Christendom with its established churches. In the United States with its religious freedom, concepts of Zion were often utilized to support the nineteenth-century effort to mold a Christian America by voluntary means. Millennialism, which appeared in many forms, a number of which undergirded the drive to prepare the way for the Lord's coming by Christianizing America, was a particularly bold prediction of the consummation of the Biblical prophecies in a near future on these shores.[9]

The idea of Zion was familiar not only to the major historic Protestant bodies, but was often seized on by religious movements that went in distinctive or dissenting directions from the Protestant mainstream. The most conspicuous illustration was provided by the Mormons, the Church of Jesus Christ of Latter-day Saints. In the

---

7. See my chapter, "Zion in American Christian Movements," in Moshe Davis, ed., *Israel: Its Role in Civilization* (New York: Harper & Bros., 1956), pp. 284-297.

8. Charles Hodge, *Systematic Theology*, 3 vols. (New York: Scribner, Armstrong & Co., 1874), 3:809.

9. See, e.g., Ernest L. Tuveson, *Redeemer Nation: The Idea of America's Millennial Role* (Chicago: University of Chicago Press, 1968); Leroy Froom, *The Prophetic Faith of Our Fathers*, 4 vols. (Washington, D.C.: Review and Herald, 1954).

Book of Mormon, it is promised by the risen Savior that for those who repent, "I will establish my church among them, and they shall come in unto the covenant and be numbered among this the remnant of Jacob, unto whom I have given this land for their inheritance. And they shall assist my people, the remnant of Jacob, and also as many of the house of Israel as shall come, that they may build a city, which shall be called the New Jerusalem" (3 Nephi 21: 22, 23). The story of the Latter-day Saints in their early years concerns the working out of their Zion ideal. By 1833 they had proceeded with such zeal and rapidity to build their Zion in Jackson County, Missouri, that the population there took alarm and had them expelled.[10] The Mormon trail then led through Nauvoo, Illinois, westward to Salt Lake City. The Zion imagery persists among the several branches of Mormonism. The Reorganized Latter-Day Saints geographically still focus around Missouri; one of their writers has said that "the burden of the message of the RLDS church to this generation is the hope of Zion in all its glory."[11] The Mormons have flourished on the American scene, but a good many of the other builders of a new Zion in America have no successors. From the founding by the Eckerling brothers of a community of Zionites on Zion Hill in eastern Pennsylvania in the colonial period to the building of Zion City, Illinois, at the dawn of the twentieth century, the list is a diverse and interesting one, and it testifies to the appeal of the Zion concept.

This transfer of Zion imagery to the American scene thus provides some interesting chapters in American church history. It has also played its role in the interrelationships of Jews and Christians. The tendency to relocate Zion has made it difficult for many Christians to understand why so many Jews have focused their thought about the Promised Land so intensely around Palestine-Israel as a part of their religious identity.

There have been through the years, however, American Christians who did not relocate Zion, but understood the Biblical prophecies to mean literally the restoration of the Jews to the Holy Land before the long-desired millennium would come. The importance of

10. See Richard L. Bushman, "New Jerusalem, U.S.A.: The Early Development of the Latter-day Saint Zion Concept on the American Frontier" (Honors Thesis in History, Harvard College, 1955).
11. T. E. Barlow, "Kingdom Emphasis," *Saints' Herald* 108 (1961).

millennial thinking in nineteenth-century Protestantism has already been mentioned; the majority of millennialists in America believed (with great variations in detail) that the spread of Christian principles would bring the glorious age into being before the return of the Lord. But there were those, whom Ernest Tuveson in a recent clarifying book has classed as "millenarians," who believed (again, with variations) that the Lord will suddenly, unexpectedly, and visibly appear in midair, that graves will be opened and vengeance visited on unbelievers as the saints are gathered in the air.[12] The millenarians usually stressed the restoration of the Jews to the Holy Land as a necessary preliminary to the second advent. In the nineteenth century there came a revival of millenarian thought, especially in the form of "dispensationalism" which developed a complex scheme of periodization. Ernest Sandeen in his book, *The Roots of Fundamentalism*, has described the work of a London barrister turned Anglican clergyman, Lewis Way, who became convinced that Biblical prophecy foretold the restoration of the Jews to Zion, and who therefore aided the cause of Palestinian resettlement. These views spread in the United States, in part through the travels of John Nelson Darby and other dispensationalists. Eventually they played a role in the rise of fundamentalism.[13]

A more indigenous form of millenarianism arose around William Miller, the adventist who prophesied the return of the Lord in 1843 or 1844. Out of the Millerite movement a number of adventist churches have arisen on the American scene. Miller believed that Christianity as a spiritual Israel had taken the place of the material Israel, and fully inherited the birthright of Israel.[14] Most other millenarians, however, clung to the other view, and were excited by the rise of the modern Zionist movement. As Sandeen summarizes a complex history: "Although confusion and controversy marked the exegesis of some aspects of their theology, no millenarians except the Millerites ever disputed the restoration of the Jews. Millenarians watched in fascination the formation of Zionism under Theodor

---

12. E.g., cf. Tuveson, *Redeemer Nation*, p. 34.
13. See Ernest L. Sandeen, *The Roots of Fundamentalism: British and American Millenarianism, 1800-1930* (Chicago: University of Chicago Press, 1970), and C. Norman Kraus, *Dispensationalism in America: Its Rise and Development* (Richmond, Va.: John Knox Press, 1958).
14. Yohah Malachy, "Seventh Day Adventists and Zionism," *Herzl Year Book* 6 (1964-1965): 265-301.

Herzl and the meeting of the first Zionist congress in Basel in 1897, and millenarians correctly, almost instinctively, grasped the significance of Allenby's capture of Jerusalem and celebrated the event as a fulfillment of prophecy."[15] In millenarian thinking, the return of the Jews to the Holy Land was preparatory to the second advent, at which time those who yielded to the returned Messiah would be gathered with him forever.

Charles Taze Russell, the founder of Jehovah's Witnesses, drew much from millenarian thought in his teaching. In 1910 he delivered a famous address to four thousand Jewish listeners at the New York Hippodrome, urging the most earnest and saintly among them to go eastward to Zion. His presses in Brooklyn poured out materials favorable to Zionism, though after his death his successor veered in quite a different direction in the 1920s.[16]

Among dispensationalists and those influenced by them the restoration motif continued to be emphasized. For example, in a book published in 1914, the Rev. I. M. Haldeman, pastor of the First Baptist Church in New York, combined humanitarian with prophetic motifs in saying that the Jew "needs to go back to his own land, go there in national capacity, and take his place amid the political and commercial powers of the earth. Not till the Jewish nation is such, not till there is a Jewish national resurrection, and the Jewish nation once more possesses the land sworn to Abraham, Isaac and Jacob, will the Jew be able to lift up his head and walk in the ordained power that is his." God has declared that this need shall be met, continued Haldeman, and has said that Israel shall be restored to Palestine. "The promises of this restoration form almost the staple of the prophetic utterances. The Word of God is crowded with them. In every form of statement, typical, figurative, poetic, symbolic, open and didactic, does the living God proclaim, by sworn oath, by solemn pledge, upon the stake of his own integrity, that his people shall yet dwell in the land of their inheritance." Haldeman showed great interest in the Zionist movement, but saw beyond the restoration to a time of troubles, after which the Lord will descend from heaven and the "repentant and sore-smitten Judah shall turn to him and own

15. Sandeen, *The Roots of Fundamentalism*, p. 234.
16. Malachy, "Jehovah's Witnesses and their Attitude toward Judaism and the Idea of the Return to Zion," *Herzl Year Book* 5 (1963-1964): 175-208.

their crucified Lord at last."[17] Here the blending of restoration and conversion motifs found a characteristic expression.

Humanitarian considerations led many Christians to support Jewish return to Palestine. The famous memorial presented to President Benjamin Harrison on 5 March 1891 by a premillennialist of Methodist background, William E. Blackstone, attracted wide attention and was signed by many prominent laymen and ministers from many denominations. Troubled over the plight of Russian Jews, Blackstone argued for the return of Palestine to the Jews. "According to God's distribution of nations it is their home—an inalienable possession from which they were expelled by force," he wrote, adding that "we believe this is an appropriate time for all nations, and especially the Christian nations of Europe, to show kindness to Israel. A million of exiles, by their terrible sufferings, are piteously appealing to our sympathy, justice, and humanity. Let us now restore to them the land of which they were so cruelly despoiled by our Roman ancestors."[18] Though the general appeal is humanitarian, in his book, *Jesus is Coming,* Blackstone presented the dispensationalist argument for the restoration.[19] Such strands in American Christian thought were among the undercurrents that fed the American sentiment of 1948 to recognize the new state of Israel when it claimed independence.

III. THE PILGRIMAGE MOTIF

Another fascinating part of the general field of America-Holy Land studies is the consideration of Americans in the past who have travelled or settled in Palestine. The complex attitudes of Americans to the Middle East have been shaped in important ways by those who have gone there as pilgrims, Biblical scholars, explorers, archaeologists, missionaries, diplomats, and tourists. It is not always easy to distinguish between the first and last; an index of secularization may well be the way modern pilgrims adopt the disguise of tourists. Men

---

17. I. M. Haldeman, *The Signs of the Times,* 5th ed. (New York: Charles C. Cook, 1914), pp. 441 f., 454.
18. *Palestine for the Jews* (Copy of memorial presented to President Harrison, 5 March 1891) (n.p., n.d.).
19. Originally published in 1878, the book went through a number of editions and many printings; by 1917 well over 350,000 copies had been printed. See Kraus, *Dispensationalism in America,* pp. 33-35.

and women of all faiths and of no professed faith have traveled and lived in the Holy Land, and of course in the twentieth century the increasing speed and relative ease of travel have escalated the numbers into unprecedented proportions. Of all who have visited the Holy Land through the centuries, I suppose the pilgrims of all kinds far outnumber the others. The stories of Christian pilgrimages from the Bordeaux Pilgrim of A.D. 333 through the accounts of missionaries like St. Willibald and the tales of the crusaders down to the letters of those who spent last Christmas in Bethlehem sometimes have surprising similarities. Now they come by jet, mingling with the faithful of other religions. The account of a famous American author of sixty years ago reminds us that it has not long been so. Henry Van Dyke wrote in 1908 about going to Jerusalem: "Hither come the innumerable companies of foot-weary pilgrims, climbing the steep roads from the sea-coast, from the Jordan, from Bethlehem—pilgrims who seek the place of the Crucifixion, pilgrims who would weep beside the walls of their vanished Temple, pilgrims who desire to pray where Mohammed prayed. Century after century these human throngs have assembled from far countries and toiled upward to this open, lofty plateau, where the ancient city rests upon the top of the closed hand, and where the ever-changing winds from the desert and the sea sweep and shift over the rocky hilltops, the mute, gray battlements, and the domes crowned with the cross, the crescent, and the star."[20] For centuries and still today the Holy Land has drawn Christians from all parts of the world like a powerful magnet; they come wanting to be at the place of Jesus' birth, to walk where he walked in Galilee, to pray in the Garden of Gethsemane, to worship at the tomb. Christians of classical Catholic and Orthodox traditions have had special interest in the holy places, while those of Reformation and evangelical traditions have often been especially concerned with deepening their understanding of the land of the Bible.

Those who have gone as pilgrims of one kind or another have often reported a mixture of feelings, a combination of disappointment and fulfillment. One of the early American visitors to the Holy Land was John Lloyd Stephens, whom Van Wyck Brooks called the

---

20. Henry Van Dyke, *Out-of-Doors in the Holy Land: Impressions of Travel in Body and Spirit* (New York: Charles Scribner's Sons, 1908), p. 50.

"greatest of American travel writers,"[21] a journalist who became something of a pilgrim in spite of himself. He wrote a paragraph which many after him were to echo in their own words: "Beginning my tour in the Holy Land at the birthplace of our Saviour, and about to follow him in his wanderings through Judea, Samaria, and Galilee, over the ground consecrated by his preaching, his sufferings, and miracles, to his crucifixion on Calvary, I must prepare my readers for a disappointment which I experienced myself. The immediate followers of our Savior, who personally knew the localities which are now guarded and reverenced as holy places, engrossed by the more important business of their Master's mission, never marked these places for the knowledge of their descendants."[22] Skepticism about the authenticity of sites reappears often in modern pilgrimage literature, and beyond that has come the realization that being at a sacred site or on a hallowed land does not necessarily bring one closer to the Holy. Yet, as many have testified, and as I can add from my own pilgrimage, something can and often does happen religiously in a unique way. For me, at Bethlehem, by the waters of Galilee, in the garden at Gethsemane, at Rachel's tomb and by the Western Wall came the almost indescribable sense of being at the meeting point of past, present, and future, and a deepening of faith that the God of history is at work among his creatures and in his creation.

Many American pilgrims experience the strange sense of familiarity, of having been there before. No doubt it was more vivid still in the days when pilgrims were more steeped in Biblical materials than many are today. When Dr. Edward Robinson approached Jerusalem in 1838 he exclaimed, "From the earliest childhood I had read of and studied the localities of this sacred spot; now I beheld them with my own eyes; and they all seemed familiar to me, as if the realization of a former dream. I seemed to be again among the cherished scenes of childhood, long unvisited, indeed, but distinctly recollected; . . ."[23]

---

21. As quoted in David H. Finnie, *Pioneers East: The Early American Experience in the Middle East* (Cambridge, Mass.: Harvard University Press, 1967), p. 6. Finnie's book is a well-written and invaluable book for study in this field; see also Teddy Kollek and Moshe Pearlman, *Pilgrims to the Holy Land: The Story of Pilgrimage Through the Ages* (New York: Harper & Row, 1970).

22. John Lloyd Stephens, *Incidents of Travel in Egypt, Arabia Petraea, and the Holy Land,* 2 vols. (New York: Harper & Bros., 1873), 2:137. Another famous travel book was written by a naval officer, commander of an American expedition to the Dead Sea, W. F. Lynch, *Narrative of the United States' Expedition to the River Jordan and the Dead Sea* (Philadelphia: Lea and Blanchard, 1849). On Lynch, see Finnie, *Pioneers East*, pp. 262-270.

23. Edward Robinson, *Biblical Researches in Palestine, Mount Sinai and Arabia Petraea. A Journal of Travels in the Year 1838 . . . ,* 3 vols. (Boston: Crocker & Brewster, 1841), 1:326.

But the sense of familiarity is soon replaced by the impact of new experiences, as the pictures, the descriptions and the maps one has seen fall into the perspective of three dimensions—perhaps more, for the dimensions of time and eternity somehow get accented here. The Bible suddenly becomes alive. The late Harry Emerson Fosdick found this to be one of the greatest values of his pilgrimage to Palestine. He exclaimed, "After years of studying the Bible I found the Book vivified and illumined by studying the country where it grew and where its major scenes were set."[24]

The real founder of the scientific study of Biblical geography [25] was the Edward Robinson mentioned above, graduate of Hamilton College and sometime teacher at Andover Seminary and later at Union Theological Seminary of New York, who journeyed through the Holy Land in 1838 and produced a massive work on Biblical topography cast in the form of a travel journal. While of course later researches led to corrections in his work, marred somewhat by an intense anti-Catholic bias, his pioneering venture in archaeology is still highly regarded. In Jerusalem he was interested in missionary work, but as he put it, "My one great object was the city itself, in its topographical and historical relations, its site, its hills, its dales, its remains of antiquity, the traces of its ancient population; in short, every thing connected with it that could have a bearing upon the illustration of the Scriptures."[26] Since Robinson, many scholars from the United States have made significant contributions to archaeological and Biblical studies, in cooperation with scholars from around the world. Here is an area of America-Holy Land studies where historians, Biblical scholars, and theologians of many faiths can work together in assessing the remarkable achievements of the past century and a half.

Scholars of other disciplines have visited the Holy Land, too. As a church historian, I have been especially interested in the work of Philip Schaff, founder of the American Society of Church History and, like Edward Robinson, one of the great figures in the history of Union Theological Seminary in New York. Schaff was seeking health and solace after a domestic crisis; his *Through Bible Lands* is a fairly

---

24. Harry Emerson Fosdick, *A Pilgrimage to Palestine* (New York: Macmillan, 1933), p. viii.
25. According to R. A. S. Macalister, *A Century of Excavation in Palestine* (New York: F. H. Revell, n.d. [1925]), pp. 21-25.
26. Robinson, *Biblical Researches*, 1:335 f.

typical, rather quick-moving travel book by a deeply learned man. Interested especially in the many types of people he met in his 1877 trip, Schaff noted how the Jews "look forward to the restoration of their race and country. Their number in Jerusalem is growing rapidly and amount fully to one third of the whole population." Commenting on the philanthropies of Baron Rothschild and Sir Moses Montefiore, Schaff believed that "they ought to buy Palestine and administer it on principles of civil and religious liberty." The distinguished historian sympathetically observed the lamentations at the Western Wall of the temple, saying, "The scene at the Wailing Place was to me touching and pregnant with meaning. God has no doubt reserved this remarkable people, which like the burning bush is never consumed, for some great purpose before the final coming of our Lord."[27]

Some of the Americans who went to the Holy Land stayed for long periods of time, many of them as missionaries. In the great surge of modern Christian missions that began toward the very end of the eighteenth century, a movement encouraged so much by the words and example of William Carey, work was undertaken in eastern Mediterranean lands, with particular attention to educational, medical, and publishing ventures. Missionaries could and did write too—outstanding among them was Dr. W. M. Thomson, for twenty-five years a member of the American Board of Commissioners for Foreign Missions, serving in Syria and Palestine. In 1859 he wrote *The Land and the Book*, which has been called "the most popular book ever written by an American missionary, and one of the best."[28] A massive two-volume work, it appeared in many editions and sold nearly 200,000 copies, apparently more than any other American book of its kind except *Uncle Tom's Cabin*. Thomson saw Palestine as "one vast tablet whereupon God's messages to men have been drawn, and graven deep in living characters by the Great Publisher of glad tidings, to be seen and read of all to the end of time. The Land and the Book—with reverence be it said—constitute the ENTIRE and ALL-PERFECT TEXT, and should be studied together."[29] Protestant missions chiefly concerned themselves with

27.. Philip Schaff, *Through Bible Lands: Notes of Travel in Egypt, the Desert, and Palestine,* new ed. (London: James Nisbet & Co., n.d. [1878]), pp. 250, 252.
28. By Finnie, *Pioneers East,* p. 187.
29. W. M. Thomson, *The Land and the Book: or, Biblical Illustrations Drawn from the Manners and Customs, the Scenes and Scenery of the Holy Land,* 2 vols. (New York: Harper & Bros., 1859), 2:xv.

attempting to revitalize "the ancient churches in the hope that they would become more active in reaching the Moslems," as Kenneth Scott Latourette put it.[30] Neither Catholic, Protestant, nor Orthodox missions have made much numerical gain among Moslems or Jews. But the impact of missionaries on the attitude of American Christians toward the Holy Land has been very great; as late as 1945 Dr. Latourette could write, "The contacts of Americans with the Near East has been predominantly through Protestant Missions." [31]

IV. TENSIONS OF TODAY

In teaching courses in church history which come down to the present day, I have noticed in my students and in myself a heightening of emotional tension as we get involved in matters with which we have close associations and personal commitments. This is especially true of America-Holy Land studies as one moves into the twentieth century, for the controversial history of Zionism—controversial for both Christians and Jews—must be taken into account. Interdisciplinary approaches to the many aspects of the establishment of the State of Israel in 1948 and subsequent developments are especially helpful. The historian needs the insights of the political scientists, the theologians, the sociologists, the social psychologists, the foreign policy experts, and the Middle East area specialists as he attempts to probe the meaning and significance of such events as the Balfour Declaration of 1917, the joint resolutions of Congress in 1922 and 1945 favoring the establishment in Palestine of a national home for the Jews, the hopes of the Palestinians during the Mandate, the deepening of Arab reaction to the trend of affairs, the impact of the Holocaust on world opinion, the United Nations resolution of 1947, the termination of the British Mandate, and the proclamation of the independence of the State of Israel on 14 May 1948, followed sixteen minutes later by recognition by the American

---

30. Kenneth Scott Latourette, *Christianity in a Revolutionary Age*, .vol. 2. *The Nineteenth Century Outside Europe: The Americas, the Pacific, Asia, and Africa* (New York: Harper & Bros., 1961), p. 396.
31. Kenneth Scott Latourette, *A History of the Expansion of Christianity*, vol. 7, *Advance Through Storm* (New York: Harper & Bros., 1945), p. 262.

government.[32] Samuel Halperin has shown in some detail how much Christian sympathy with the general Zionist aim there was in the 1940s, concluding that "these abundant manifestations of Christian concurrence with Zionist objectives are all the more impressive in the face of the relative paucity of anti-Zionist expression by non-Jews. Anti-Zionist Christian sentiment, which later found a home in the American Friends of the Middle East, was not widely articulated by notable groups or even individual statesmen before 1948." Halperin finds that "expressions of Christian Zionist sentiment were both genuine and indigenous to the American culture."[33] Some of the backgrounds for attempting to understand such expressions have been sketched in this paper.

Many Christians had reservations, however, which soon found expression, especially as to the plight of Arab refugees following the outbreak of war in 1948. To pick a single example, Millar Burrows, a noted Biblical scholar, published a book in 1949 which declared that "in this book I shall sincerely try to be fair to both sides. Strongly as I feel that Zionism is basically and tragically wrong, I shall endeavor to express my convictions in such a way that Jewish friends, whom I respect and admire but with whom I profoundly differ on this question, will at least feel that I am honest and moved by worthy motives." He went on to call attention to the wrong done to the Arabs of Palestine, and to the vexing refugee problem, concluding that "the best case that can be made for Zionism is not good enough to justify the wrong done by the establishment of a Jewish state in Palestine."[34] Other Christians took the other side; Carl Hermann Voss, again to pick a single example, wrote a book on the thesis that "the establishment of Israel was and is a creative answer to the world problem of anti-Semitism—an answer which might not be absolutely just to Arab rights in Palestine, but which seemed just in view of the granting of sovereignty to so many Arab states throughout the

---

32. The bibliography in this field is vast; cf. e.g., Nadav Safran, *The United States and Israel* (Cambridge, Mass.: Harvard University Press, 1963); Carl J. Friedrich, *American Policy toward Palestine* (Washington, D.C.: Public Affairs Press, 1944); Frank E. Manuel, *The Realities of American-Palestine Relations* (Washington, D.C.: Public Affairs Press, 1949); and Selig Adler, "Backgrounds of American Policy Toward Zion," in Davis, ed., *Israel: Its Role in Civilization*, pp. 251-283.
33. Samuel Halperin, *The Political World of American Zionism* (Detroit: Wayne State University Press, 1961), pp. 186 f.
34. Millar Burrows, *Palestine Is Our Business* (Philadelphia: Westminster Press, 1949), pp. 13 f.

Middle East."[35] So the debate has gone on, intensified by the events of the 1967 war.[36]

The Christian of scholarly temperament who seeks to promote peace through disciplined study can work with those of various fields and faiths who need not forsake their commitments to religion or to justice but who will seek to shed light where there is inevitably much heat. My own experience in joint seminars shows it can be done; often this tangled period can be approached by focusing on the way some particular leader of thought and action has moved through the stormy scene. In probing the most difficult areas, I have found tested but respected such beliefs of mine as the safeguarding of the right of the State of Israel to continued existence and the giving of fair recognition to the rights of Palestinians. In the continuing scholarly discussion of America and the Holy Land I am convinced that there must be a developing partnership not only between Christians and Jews, but also with an involvement of Arab thinkers. In my own continuing work in America-Holy Land studies, I hope to get involved more than I yet have with both Christian and Muslim Arab scholars. There are some signs of hope; in Jerusalem a "Rainbow Group" brings Christians and Jews into a continuing dialogue; F. Dean Lueking in *The Christian Century* about a year ago reported on a fascinating and hopeful exchange in Chicago on Israel between a Jewish scholar and an Arab Christian leader of Galilee; and a recent World Council of Churches publication reports that a working party of Christians, Muslims, and Jews found it could have fruitful contacts on a religious level, and found a basis for reconciliatory action.[37]

During the last decade, interfaith cooperation has been vastly enriched through what is clearly one of the major events in the long history of the church, the Second Vatican Council. Though not completely satisfactory to all, the statements concerning religious liberty in general and relating to Jews in particular have broken new

---

35. Carl Hermann Voss, *The Palestine Problem Today: Israel and Its Neighbors* (Boston: Beacon Press, 1953), p. 13.
36. See, e.g., A. Roy and Alice Eckardt, "Again Silence in the Churches," *The Christian Century* 84 (2 August 1967): 992-995; Y. Malachy, "The Christian Churches and the Six Day War," *The Weiner Library Bulletin* 23:14-25; Krister Stendahl, "Judaism and Christianity: II—After a Colloquium and a War," *Harvard Divinity Bulletin* 32 (Autumn 1967): 1-8.
37. F. Dean Lueking, "Hopeful Voices from Israel," *The Christian Century* 87 (4 February 1970): 139-141; World Council of Churches, "The Church and the Jewish People," *Newsletter No. 3* (September 1970), p. 5.

ground and have helped to reduce some of the traditional misunderstandings. There is need now for a fuller exploration of historic attitudes of American Roman Catholics toward the Holy Land. In this country, the Bishops' Committee for Ecumenical and Inter-religious Affairs issued a policy statement in 1967 which called (among other things) for "scholarly studies and educational effort to show the common historical, biblical, doctrinal, and liturgical heritage shared by Catholics and Jews, as well as the differences." [38] As part of such studies and efforts, cooperative scholarship in the field of America-Holy Land studies can make significant contributions.

---

38. As quoted in Oesterreicher, ed., *Brothers in Hope*, p. 261. For the Second Vatican Council's "Declaration on the Relationship of the Church to Non-Christian Religions"'and "Declaration on Religious Freedom," see Walter J. Abbott, ed., *The Documents of Vatican II* (New York: Guild Press, America Press, Association Press, 1966), pp. 656-700.

Have Jews and Christians a Common Future?

FRANKLIN H. LITTELL

The original plan for this essay was a dissertation of "The interrupted dialogue between Christians and Jews," a very real and painful aspect of the present confusion. But such a study could only be morphological and it is the view of the future which shapes "the present moment" in its limitations and possibilities. Therefore, the subject has been re-stated to accent the eschatological note, which provides *the* interesting historical question for all but antiquarians.

This presentation grows out of immediate experience in the classroom on two fronts. First, in teaching the basic course in Church History I have emphasized three major dimensions: doctrines, social teachings, and expansion; a secondary emphasis on the relations of Christians and Jews has been just as rewarding of new insights and useful lessons. Second, in connection with ten years of a graduate seminar entitled "Contemporary Church History: The Encounter with Totalitarianism," I have come to see hatred of the Jews as a constant factor in the recurrent breakdowns of Christianity into a baser religious element. It is almost always present in the dynamic anti-Christian ideologies and movements of this age of totalitarianism, and it is a covert force—irrupting into overt expression throughout the entire history of Christendom. The answer to Jules Isaac's famous question: "Is Christianity Necessarily Anti-Semitic?" must be affirmative if by "Christianity" we mean the religio-cultural monolith which was Christendom for fifteen centuries.[1]

This study arises, therefore, out of a lively concern for the present state of Christianity as well as a desire to understand better the grandeur and misery of its past. If the possibility for understanding

---

This article was originally presented 26 October 1969 at the Annual Meeting of the American Academy of Religion in Boston, Massachusetts.

1. Jules Isaac, *Has Anti-Semitism Roots in Christianity?* (New York: National Conference of Christians and Jews, 1961); see also Isaac's *The Teaching of Contempt* (New York: Holt, Rinehart and Winston, 1964).

and cooperation between Christians and Jews is one of the peculiar potentials of the American system of religious liberty and pluralism, we should be keenly aware that when Christian culture-religion slides into its more demonic expressions the hatred of the Jews comes to the fore. Most of us have some awareness of the truth that the Nazis' murder of six million Jews in our own lifetime was a traumatic event in the history of Christianity as well as the history of the Jewish people. We should also be aware that the leaders of our religious underworld in America, in their resistance to the process of secularization and sponsorship of reactionary programs to reconstitute a mythical "Christian America," are likewise anti-Semitic.

I

The term "anti-Semitic" is unsatisfactory for several reasons. It was popularized as a term to categorize a certain type of intolerance in early nineteenth-century humanitarian discussions pointing towards cultural and political assimilation of Jews into the life of the enlightened Christian nations of Western Europe. Today our anthropology is more advanced and our experience of the demonic dimension of ideologies and political programs based on hatred of the Jews is more agonizing. The term "anti-Semitism," moreover, blurs the degree to which hatred of the Jews is endemic in Muslim culture and civilization in the same way as it is in Christendom. (Muslim "anti-Semitism," which led some key leaders openly to sympathize with Hitler and Nazism and has in recent decades fired the Holy War—jihad—against Israel, needs a great deal more study and analysis than it has yet received.) The real issue before us is theological, not humanitarian at all. The crux of the matter is hatred of the Jews who—whether they are personally believers or not—are a sign in history to the One who is both Author and Judge of development and meaning in human events.

Alienation between Christians and Jews began early. It is not a product of the modern age, although modern science made possible its more demonic consequences. It began, in fact, in the failure of the Church Fathers to handle adequately the encounter with Judaism. This is not the time to discuss the question raised by some contemporary exegetes and theologians: Are there New Testament passages which justify hatred of the Jews? Professor Roy Eckardt, in his brilliant treatise, *The Elder and Younger Brothers,*[2] and in one of the articles in this volume, has summarized that discussion. The point is that the Church Fathers who so competently dealt with the mystery religions, Zoroastrianism, Stoicism, and the like—failed in their treatment of the Jewish heritage and prepared the way for later tragedy. Nothing but the bitterness of a family quarrel would seem to explain the hideous language of Cyprian, Justin Martyr, Origen, Jerome, Chrysostom, et al. in reference to God's first Israel. Of course the inflated verbiage of late classical rhetoric accounts for some of the phrases, but in any case their handling of the Judaic heritage was anything but an intellectual triumph.

As the official religion of the empire after Constantine, Christianity abandoned the imagery of covenant and pilgrimage and cultivated the uses of religion as social cement and political sanction. Only a few critical spirits, chiefly in the monastic orders, retained the image of the earthly pilgrim. Otherwise the sign was identified with the spectral myth of the "wandering Jew," cursed for "deicide" and condemned to be scattered far from the homeland. In fact, large numbers of Jews sought refuge from the savageries of the culture-Christians in the Persian Empire and as far away as India. Christians settled in, leaving pilgrimage to the Jews: only recently has the image of a pilgrimage church come back into Catholic thought.

The Jews suffered grievously under Christendom, in normal times being subject to political and economic discrimination and in times of excitement being burned out and murdered. As might be expected, just as the ablest Roman Emperors were the worst persecutors of the Christians, so the ablest princes in Christendom were the worst persecutors of the Jews. One of the worst series of events of mob violence came with the First Crusade, when the crowds pressing southward to fight the Turks turned aside to murder the internal "enemies," the Jews. Innocent III, who unleashed the Dominicans on the Albigenses and persecuted the Bogomils so savagely that they became converts to Islam, introduced the requirement that Jews wear the yellow Star of David in public. Two centuries later, the same pious intent which led Ferdinand and Isabella to finance Christian conquest of the New World also pointed them toward savage suppression of Jewry in Spain. Catholics,

---

2. A. Roy Eckardt, *The Elder and Younger Brothers* (New York: Charles Scribner's Sons, 1967), chap. 7.

Lutherans, and Orthodox, however divided by doctrinal disputes and wars of religion at the time of the Reformation, were united in oppression of the Jews. The "pale" of Jewish Settlement in Eastern Europe, within which Jews were restricted from 1791 until the end of Russian Tsardom, remained into the twentieth century a visible expression of Christendom's endemic hatred of the Jews. In periods of excitement when the peasants became restless under their oppressors, Tsarist rulers and Orthodox priests cooperated in diverting popular resentment toward the Jews; until the time of Hitler, Bormann, and Eichmann, the pogroms in Tsarist Russia (which among other things resulted in great emigrations of East European Jews to the U.S.A.) were the most cruel of Christendom's anti-Jewish frenzies in the modern age.

The Reformer Martin Luther turned to a vile attack on the Jews in his embittered last years. Balthasar Hübmaier, in the beginnings of his own struggle to develop the program of radical church reform which eventually led him to Anabaptism, appealed to mob support by attacks on the Jews. Only Calvinism, with its strong reliance on the Old Testament and covenant theology broke the mold. Oliver Cromwell readmitted Jews to the England from which they had been driven shortly after Innocent III's Fourth Lateran Council, and various philo-Semitic movements emerged in radical Puritanism which deliberately adopted Old Testament symbols and turned against Rome and Canterbury and toward Jerusalem. Since that time there have been many radical Protestant sects which have worked to reconstitute the Israel of God, pitted against the heathen or Gentiles. Not all of them, in reclaiming ancient ground, have however escaped anti-Semitism: the Anglo Israelite cult would be an example of this.

The Enlightenment and the French Revolution softened Western Christian nations toward assimilation of the Jews. Christendom as a whole was not affected, however, as the Dreyfus case in France and the Leo Frank case in Georgia and the Holocaust in modern Germany amply document. Even some rather enlightened Biblical scholars and theologians have been anti-Semites, as their negative references to the Judaic heritage of Christianity clearly show, although today few would be guilty of the crime in its political and vulgar forms. Christendom, as such studies of basic Christian literature as *Faith and Prejudice* by Bernhard Olsen[3] and *Les Juifs*

---

3. Bernhard E. Olsen, *Faith and Prejudice* (New Haven: Yale University Press, 1963).

dans la Catéchèse by Abbe François Houtart et al.[4] amply document, remains endemically anti-Semitic. This was the issue on which Vatican II failed miserably. This is the issue on which the American Protestant establishment is most insensitive.

Yet the constitutional conditions of the U.S.A., with the development of religious liberty, voluntaryism, and pluralism, are favorable to a new level of Christian-Jewish encounter. "Only in America," where the religious covenants and political covenant have been separated in principle since the great Bill of Religious Freedom in Virginia (1786) and the First Amendment to the Federal Constitution (1789-1791), is it possible for fellow-citizens of church and synagogue to attempt a new level of dialogue and understanding. There can only be a genuine dialogue where government is secular and no citizen subject to discrimination or repression because of religious opinions (or lack of them). As a matter of fact, with Catholic and Jewish and Protestant communities at the height of their strength in attendance and support and membership, dialogue and interfaith cooperation have become the chief planks of social progress in the American scene.

We are now entering a time, however, in which the chances of retrogression are very great. Nativism of the fascist type is on the rise and so is overt hatred of the Jews. In this crisis nothing is more contributory than a fatal flaw in liberal Protestant theology. It is daily more painfully clear that not only have the American churches failed to work through the significance of the Holocaust for church history, but in their indiscipline and comfortable status as social establishments they are in some respects closer to European Christendom than to the Free Church standards which are their heritage. They do not persecute so much as they maintain indifference to persecution and harrassment by others—who often give overt expression to their own covert prejudices.

II

Since 1958 there has been a marked rise of the Radical Right in American politics, accompanied in most cases by overt anti-Semitism. In 1961 something less than $1 million went into the work

---

4. Francois Houtart et al., *Les Juifs dans la Catechèse* (Louvain: Centre de Récherches Socio-Religieuses, 1969).

of the John Birch Society and its associated enterprises; in 1968, the figure was between $46 million and $50 million with a great deal of it in corporation subsidy. The same kind of reasoning which led Krupp and Thyssen to finance the Nazis is now exhibited by Cinemacolor, Schick Eversharp, Allen-Bradley, and numerous others in their underwriting of the Radical Right. The popular myth, signalized by Dirksen's Prayer Amendment and Hargis' Christian Crusade, is a return to "Christian America." Reactionaries, some even in Congress, have joined with the leaders of our guerillas to resist America's shift from WASP hegemony to the pluralism which the Constitution implies. All of our major church boards and agencies, as well as the National Council of Churches and other ecumenical organs, have felt increasingly the effect of a barrage of radio and TV propaganda from the extremists of the right. The failure of most of them to meet the challenge head-on has encouraged the insolence of the McIntires, Hargises, McBirnies, Cottons, and Perlos, and it has left Jewish agencies like the Anti-Defamation League and the American Jewish Committee— which acted immediately to withstand this drive for power—exposed to the brunt of the attack.[5]

A second factor which has served to drive a rift between Jews and Christians, and to make the dialogue increasingly difficult, was the calm indifference with which church agencies viewed the Arab League's attempted second Holocaust in their third attack on Israel—the so-called Six-Day War of 1967. It would be diversionary to dwell too long on the situation in the Middle East, and there are a number of positions which can be argued either way without disturbing the central thesis of this paper. But it may be recalled that German propagandists in 1938-1941, echoed faithfully by some American isolationists, accused Jews in America of meddling in the internal affairs of the Third Reich when they urged the U.S. government to intervene politically on behalf of those to be slaughtered in Auschwitz, Theresienstadt, Bergen-Belsen, and other centers of modern science. Our newspapers are full of parallel ads and letters today, attacking American Jews for their sense of identification with those who escaped and now fall again at the hands of an implacable and racist foe. At least this much can be

5. Franklin H. Littell, *Wild Tongues: A Handbook of Social Pathology* (New York: Macmillan Co., 1969).

asked: Are American Jews to be faulted today because they expect churchmen to take more than casual interest in the same programs—launched in part by some of Hitler's allies and supporters—against the refugees who have managed to survive, resettle, and build up the new nation of Israel? Was the first Holocaust simply an event in Jewish history, which civilized Gentiles must regret in the same way they regret white brutality toward the Cherokees, Cheyennes, and Nez Perces, or was it an event in *Christian* history? Jewish leaders in America like Eliezer Berkowitz and Marc Tanenbaum have expressed publicly what the whole Jewish community feels, namely, such insensitivity and opaqueness raises doubts about the whole value of the Christian-Jewish dialogue, and the sincerity with which it is approached by American churchmen.

On 7 July 1967 the General Board of the National Council of Churches issued a statement of serene objectivity which was noteworthy for its failure to mention the two most important factors in the whole attack on Israel: the theological meaning of the Holocaust and the threatened second Holocaust; and the Russian role in equipping and releasing the attack. A different statement came from the Dutch Council of Churches, whose members have experienced before the political diabolism which hatred of the Jews can inspire and whose theology has taken the first Holocaust into account and did not stop with the nineteenth century.

Since 1967 the Russians have poured another two billion dollars of equipment into the area, and another "Holy War" is impending. Is the proposed slaughter of another 2.5 million Jews merely a political issue for the Gentiles, or have Christians *as Christians* something to say and do about the hatred of the Jews so endemic in Christendom (and Muslim civilization)? Karl Barth in *The Church and the Political Problem of our Day*[6] was dealing with precisely this issue in challenging those to whom Nazi racism and murder were also "merely political" issues.

This brings us to the theological problem, and the necessity of rebuilding the trust which alone might enable open-faced dialogue between Christians and Jews. The immediate argument is clear, although negative in direction: the rise of the anti-Christian ideologies and movements which are the mark on the forehead of the

---

6. Karl Barth, *The Church and the Political Problem of our Day* (New York: Charles Scribner's Sons, 1939).

twentieth century is a threat to both church and synagogue. Jews bear the brunt of the assault for a very concrete reason: few of them can take on protective coloration and disappear. The baptized Gentiles, on the other hand, who are only spiritual Semites, can betray their baptism, apostatize, and back out of history into the tribe, into the nothingness from which they were once called into being. The tragedy of twentieth century church history is that under temptation or pressure tens of millions of the baptized have done just that—embracing the Teutonic folk myths, the Anglo-Saxon tribalism, the romantic pan-Slavism of their natural state. Their hatred of the Jews, and toward the author and judge of history to whom they remain a sign, becomes overt; their hatred of the Jew Jesus of Nazareth may remain hidden, although "true believers" of the calibre of Martin Bormann do not hesitate there either. The awesome mystery of this age is the truth that the six million Jews who perished in twentieth-century Christendom died for the God of Abraham, Isaac, and Jacob—who is also the God of the baptized, for whom they, too, would suffer and die had they stayed true to their baptism. To speak paradoxically, most of the martyrs for Jesus Christ in this century were Jews, although some baptized Gentiles like Dietrich Bonhoeffer and Father Alfred Delp and Helmuth von Moltke also paid the final price of their place and time in history.

When the Gentiles apostatize, they commonly turn to hatred of the Jews. Why is *Kultur-religion* so endemically anti-Semitic, and in its demonic moments overtly so? Eric Voegelin, in his classic *Israel and Revelation,* has given a full explanation of this phenomenon—and at the same time has exposed to the naked eye the covert cultural anti-Semitism of such a writer as Arnold Toynbee—to whose lofty thirty-six thousand possible cycles of civilization the Biblical view of history must always be offensive, the superstitious myths of a "Semitic fossil" (Toynbee's term for the Jewish people).[7] The argument may be summarized as follows: In all pre-Biblical systems the function of religion is to act as the cement of society, and the gods are there to serve the tribe. The priestly caste is trained to bring the gods into focus as needed, particularly in political or military crises; even certain tricks are used and remembered, to that end. The religious "leap in being"[8] came when at Sinai the god who is God

---

7. Eric Bogelin, *Order and History, I: Israel and Revelation* (Baton Rouge: Louisiana State University Press, 1956), p. 210.
8. Ibid., p. 123.

issued the charter for a new people, created from the Hebrews and
the tag-ends of other tribes; their charter of existence was to do His
will. Christians believe that this covenant, of God's election rather
than ethnic identity, was confirmed in Jesus Christ and that in time
men of all tribes and tongues and races receive a new identity. Since,
however, human material is very refractory, those baptized into
history have across the centuries of Christendom repeatedly reverted
to the heathen style of attempting to accommodate God to tribal
gods and purposes. This process has been evident in culture-religion,
such as that of Victorian England and *das Wilhelminische Zeitalter*—
not to mention the set of myths signalized by the term "Christian
America," and it is a major force in such artificial tribal religions as
Nazism, fascism, Falangisme, and the creed of the Ku Klux Klan.
Pan-Slavism has also been a major factor in the Communism of East
Europe, as Professor Cornelius Krahn has recently shown.[9] When the
baptized retreat into tribal religion, they abandon history in the
Biblical sense, and hatred of the Jews is often the first and most
dependable seismographic reading on the shaking of the foundations
and impending betrayal of Christ and His work of human
redemption.

Religious liberty, the separation of the political and religious
covenants, given Constitutional status in the First Amendment and
interpretative decisions of the Supreme Court, not only implies Free
Churches, it defines "secular" government. Secular government, one
of the greatest achievements in the history of human liberty, is
government which leaves to the churches and synagogues all matters
pertaining to the ultimate loyalties of men. In spite of the tendency
of reactionary politicians to try to resist the process of secularization, in spite of foot-faulting by political and religious authorities
who fear and resent secularity, such evidence as the changed status of
conscientious objection to war between World War I and the present
would indicate that government at its best is restrained, conducted in
a low tone of voice, and self-understood to be secular (theologically
speaking, "creaturely"). Secular government, and the absence of legal
sanctions or penalties for religious opinions (or lack of them), is a
very important theological or church historical development—in no

---

9. Cornelius Krahn, "Russia: Messianism-Marxism," *The Journal of Bible and Religion* 31
(July 1963): 210-219.

sense a "merely political" phenomenon.[10] For Jews and Christians, religious liberty creates the conditions—very new in the scale of centuries—for open-faced dialogue. It also, like the development of missions by the renewal movements of Hinduism, Buddhism, and Islam,[11] affords the basis for an uninhibited dialogue between other high religions. It is also well for Christians to remember that, as our best Protestant theologian of Christian-Jewish relations, A. Roy Eckardt, has pointed out, an awful fate for Christians as well as Jews would be to have to live again in a "Christian state," when triumphalism and intolerance could once more prosper.[12]

Jews and Christians thus have an ample basis for theological dialogue—in the tragedy of the Holocaust, in the common adversary appearing in the ideologies and movements of twentieth century totalitarianism, and in the still rather unique American experiment in religious voluntaryism and secular government. Wherein lies the fundamental difficulty?

Apart from the psychological impediments to which reference was earlier made, the answer to the question would seem to lie in the peculiar character of American Jewish and Christian leadership. And here I must write as a Protestant, leaving to Catholic colleagues to discuss the problem as it relates to their own communion.

First, American Protestantism is by and large Marcionite in its view of the Old Testament and its relation to the Jewish heritage. Even churches not conspicuously embedded in the nineteenth-century liberal philosophy are still wont to drive a sharp wedge between the Old Testament and the New Testament and to distinguish sharply the acts of the merciful God of the New Testament from the acts of the righteous and judgmental God of the Old Testament. As Canon Oliver C. Quick long ago pointed out in his classical study of *Liberalism, Modernism and Tradition*, this radical break between Old Testament and New Testament is the distinguishing feature of the "liberal" attitude to Church History.[13]

10. Franklin H. Littell, *The Church and the Body Politic* (New York: Seabury Press, 1968), chap. 6.

11. Kurt Hutten and Siegfriedon Kortzfleisch, eds., *Asien Missioniert im Abendland* (Stuttgart: Kreuz-Verlag, 1962).

12. A. Roy Eckardt, "The Jewish-Christian Encounter: Six Guidelines for a New Relationship," offprint from the *Journal* of the Central Conference of American Rabbis for June 1948, p. 30.

13. Oliver C. Quick, *Liberalism, Modernism and Tradition* (London: Longmans, Green and Co. 1922), p. 4f.

Contemporaries may be surprised to hear it, but in this sense most sectarian Protestantism from Menno Simons to the present has helped to create the mindset which can accommodate to *Deutsches Christentum* and other hyphenated forms of Christian tribal religion. To emphasize a radical break between Old Testament and New Testament is to prepare the way for an "Aryan" Christ, spiritualized out of his historical setting and historical work, and for another *Alttestament*. As Professor J. L. Hromadka expressed it: "The liberal theology in Germany and in her orbit utterly failed. It was willing to compromise on the essential points of divine law and of 'the law of nature'; to dispose of the Old Testament and to accept the law of the Nordic race instead; and to replace the 'Jewish' law of the Old Testament by the autonomous law of each race and nation respectively. It had made all the necessary preparation for the 'Germanization of Christianity' and for a racial Church."[14]

Friedrich Murawski, a prominent spokesman for the German Christians, drew the logical conclusions from the liberal scholars' rejection of the Jewish Old Testament:

All theologians, as far as they think in a scholarly fashion, are in agreement concerning all these things. This means from a *theological standpoint* one cannot distinguish between the *Jewish* legends and any others. Whereby the question is raised again: If they are *only* legends—why then Jewish ones of all things?

When the influential *teachers of the church* reject in their scholarly *publications* the entirety of the "historical" Bible as mere fiction, when they do not even stop at the founders of the church, when they prove wrong the central points of church life, when, according to their presentation, the Bible has absolutely no more meaning than a book of fairy tales—should not a German of the twentieth century once and for all renounce both *for himself and his children* the myths of the Near East and the Jewish church, in order to choose instead *his own* myth which is an outgrowth of *his own* blood, *his own* worldview, *his own* life style: the myth of the twentieth century?[15]

Why not indeed, if the Old Testament is but Jewish folklore and fable and without any final authority for Christians, should baptized Teutons or Anglo-Saxons or blacks or Arabs hesitate to put forth their own tribal history as *Alttestament?* The so-called Near East missionary center at Beirut, one of the major centers of anti-Semitic

---

14. J. L. Hromadka, *Doom and Resurrection* (Richmond: John Knox Press, 1945), p. 102.
15. Fredrich Murawski, *Die politische Kirche und ihre biblischen "Urkunden"* (Berlin: Theodor Fritsch Verlag, 1938), pp. 18, 95.

propaganda in the world today, has given just as clear an answer to
this question as ever did Professor Cajus Fabricius, Nazi theologian in
Berlin, in his book entitled *Positives Christentum.*[16] Major representatives of the American Protestant churches have shown quite
clearly how squarely they take their stand on the same theological
ground as the *Deutsche Christen* in the fateful years 1933-1936.

On the Jewish side, the Orthodox have never engaged in dialogue
and the Conservatives are reserved. Only Reform Judaism has been
prominent in cooperative ventures, and its rabbis were until the
Holocaust as completely children of the Enlightenment as liberal
Protestant churchmen. In all cultural and community affairs, the
leadership of the liberal rabbis is invaluable; in many American cities
the Temple is the major center of civilization, and generous Jewish
laymen are a chief support of church-related colleges and universities.
But where do we find teaching and writing dealing with the future of
Christians and Jews at the theological level? In the *Jewish
Encyclopedia*[17] published before the First World War, we find under
"Eschatology" the following argument: The mission of Judaism is to
work parallel to Christianity, with its missionary outreach to the
world's peoples, and to bring all eventually to worship of a service to
the One True God. (This "mission" was defined at Pittsburgh in
1885.) Where shall we find the equivalent to that view stated today
by Jewish teachers?

The nub of the matter is that neither Christians nor Jews are
availing themselves of the opportunity, indeed the necessity, for
theological dialogue in depth. And liberal Protestant scholars, who
have been the first to enjoy and explore the blessings of free inquiry
in religion, commonly discuss the problem at the same level as
tension and conflict between Scots-Irish and Irish, Japanese and
Koreans.

For reasons which should be clear by now, I believe a far closer
alliance with the Jewish communities and deeper study of the Judaic
heritage to be the single most important specific to cure American
Protestantism's sickness. It is useless to talk about Grace without the
background in the Law. Dietrich Bonhoeffer's whole discourse on
"cheap grace" is relevant here. It is meaningless, indeed dangerous, to
affirm the individualism of religious choice without a deep commit-

---

16. Cajus Fabricius, *Positives Christentum im neuen staat* (Dresden: H. Püschel, 1936).
17. Isidore Singer, ed., *Jewish Encyclopedia* (New York: Funk and Wagnalls Co., 1925).

ment to an abiding historic community. Martin Buber's *Two Types of Faith*[18] speaks to our conditions here. It is destructive of all worthy experience and learning to stress history as *Kairos* to the exclusion of *Chronos,* the other pole of the dialectic.

To put the matter in a form which sums up the argument from history and moral imperative of this time and place, let me use this form of words: It is God's manifest intent that the Jews and the Christians be inextricably interlocked in the historical process, and it is here proposed that neither can be saved without the other. Whether we like it or not, Jews and Christians share a common future. A "final solution to the Jewish problem," such as effected in the first Holocaust and attempted in the second, would if consummated mean not only the end of the Jews but the end of Christianity in any but a sham or apostate form. By the same token, dynamic interaction and cooperation between Christians and the Jewish people will contribute to the religious renewal of the people of both communities.

---

18. Martin Buber, *Two Types of Faith: The Interpenetration of Judaism and Christianity,* trans. N. P. Goldhawk (New York: Harper and Row, 1961).

A Selected and Annotated Bibliography on Jewish–Christian Relations

JAMES E. WOOD, JR.

THIS BIBLIOGRAPHY does not include those publications written on or as an introduction to Judaism and/or Christianity, but rather contains volumes having expressly to do with *relations* between Judaism and Christianity or Jews and Christians.

Abrahams, Israel. *Jewish Life in the Middle Ages.* New York: Meridian Books, 1958. Many printings have appeared since this work was originally published in 1896 by a renowned scholar. A panorama of the little-known, rich, social, and cultural life of the Jews during this period.

———. *Studies in Pharisaism and the Gospels.* Cambridge: University of Cambridge Press, 1917-1924. Originally designed as an appendix to C. G. Montefiore's commentary on the synoptic gospels, this work profoundly altered scholarly understanding of the character and development of the Pharisaic movement.

Adler, Michael. *Jews of Medieval England.* London: Jewish Historical Society of England, 1939. An account of the political, religious, and social conditions affecting Jewry in England during the Middle Ages.

Agus, Jacob Bernard. *Dialogue and Tradition: The Challenges of Contemporary Judeo-Christian Thought.* New York: Abelard-Schuman, 1971. The author seeks to provide the response of Judaism to the major challenges of the modern world. Part One of this volume is expressly devoted to "The Jewish-Christian Dialogue," which includes a Jewish response to Daniélou's *Dialogue with Israel* and Bea's *The Church and the Jewish People.*

Allport, Gordon W. *The Nature of Prejudice.* Cambridge, Mass.: Addison-Wesley, 1954. A major study of prejudices and antipathies which reveals that such social phenomena throughout history have had little to do with race, but rather have been based "often on religion," a prime example of which is the treatment accorded Jews in Western societies; researches and illustrations are drawn largely from the United States.

Aron, Robert. *The Jewish Jesus.* Maryknoll, N.Y.: Orbis Books, 1971. A portrait of Jesus seen in the socio-religious context of his daily practice of the Jewish faith "he knew and loved"; contains an anthology of Hebrew prayers—prayers which the young Jesus said and prayers which are still recited and sung in Jewish homes and synagogues throughout the world.

Baeck, Leo. *Judaism and Christianity.* Philadelphia: Jewish Publication Society, 1958. Examines various aspects of Judaism and Christianity, noting the Jewish influences on Christianity as well as the differences in emphases between the two faiths. Included are essays on "The Faith of Paul" and "The Gospel as a Document of the History of the Jewish Faith."

Baer, Yitzhak. *A History of the Jews in Christian Spain.* Translated from the Hebrew by Louis Schoffman. 2 vols. Philadelphia: Jewish Publication Society of America, 1961. A translation of the second Hebrew edition, but contains material not found in either of the Hebrew editions; a definitive work.

Balthasar, Hans Urs. von. *Martin Buber and Christianity: A Dialogue Between Israel and the Church.* New York: Macmillan Co., 1962. A Roman Catholic study of Judaism and its relations with Christianity and Christianity's relations with Judaism.

Barth, Markus. *Israel and the Church: Contribution to a Dialogue Vital for Peace.* Richmond, Va.: John Knox Press, 1969. The author attempts to renew the conversation between Jews and Christians by directly dealing with such questions as: What can a Jew believe about Jesus—and still remain a Jew? Was Paul an anti-Semite? The difficulty with the Pauline writings lies in the Christian understanding of Paul rather than in Paul himself or in Jewish interpretation. The final section, "Israel and the Church in Paul's Epistle to the Ephesians," shows how Ephesians can throw light on the problem of Christian usage of the Old Testament, the mission to the Jews, and Christian responsibility in regard to hidden or manifest anti-Semitism.

Baum, Gregory. *Is the New Testament Anti-Semitic?* Rev. ed. Glen Rock, N.J.: Paulist Press, 1965. Author argues that the New Testament is without anti-Semitic elements.

——————. *The Jews and the Gospel: A Re-examination of the New Testament.* Westminster, Md.: Newman Press, 1961. Examines, in the light of the Gospels, Acts, and Pauline writings, the relation between the synagogue and the early church during the first century. This study is a reply to Jules Isaac's *Jesus and Israel.*

Bea, Augustin Cardinal. *The Church and the Jewish People.* New York: Harper and Row, 1966. A commentary on the Second Vatican Council's "Declaration on the Relation of the Church to Non-Christian Religions"; written by the Council's architect of the "Declaration on the Jewish People," which was passed by Vatican II in its final session.

Bird, Thomas E., ed. *Modern Theologians, Christians and Jews.* New York: Association Press, 1967; Notre Dame, Ind.: University of Notre Dame Press, 1967. Ten studies by a variety of Christian and Jewish theologians, including, among others, such "Theologians of Dialogue" as Martin Buber, John Courtney Murray, and Josef Hromadka, and "Theologians of Mystical Experience" as Abraham Joshua Heschel and Henry de Lubas.

Blumstock, Robert Edward. *The Evangelization of Jews: A Study of Interfaith Relations.* Eugene: University of Oregon, 1964. Originally written as a doctoral dissertation in sociology for the University of Oregon.

Bokser, Ben Zion. *Judaism and the Christian Predicament.* New York: Alfred A. Knopf, 1967. A historical and critical study of the common origins as well as the crucial non-negotiable differences between Judaism and Christianity.

Borowitz, Eugene et al. *Image of the Jews: Teacher's Guide to Jews and Their Religion.* New York: Anti-Defamation League of B'nai B'rith, 1970. Prepared as the first extensive body of instructional material on Judaism for the Catholic high school, but could well be used for social studies by all religious denominations, as well as by public schools.

Brandon, Samuel George F. *The Fall of Jerusalem and the Christian Church: A Study of the Effects of the Jewish Overthrow of 70 A.D. on Christianity.* New York: Macmillan Co., 1951. A study of the primitive and early church against the background of Jewish history from 586 B.C.-70 A.D.

Branscomb, Bennett Harvie. *Jesus and the Law of Moses.* London: Hodder & Stoughton, 1930. A Biblical study of the relation of the Gospels to the Old Testament, particularly as seen in the teachings of Jesus.

Bratton, Fred Gladstone. *The Crime of Christendom: The Theological Sources of Christian Anti-Semitism.* Boston: Beacon Press, 1969. This volume on anti-Semitism was necessitated, according to the author, "because of the almost total failure of modern writers on the subject to recognize the critical significance of religious beliefs as a prominent source for secular anti-semitism." The sources of Christian anti-Semitism are seen as stemming from the anti-Jewish bias of the New Testament, the teachings of the Church Fathers, and the continuance of certain Christological formulations in official creeds, literature, religious education, and preaching in the life of the churches themselves.

Buber, Martin. *Two Types of Faith: The Interpenetration of Judaism and Christianity.* Translated by Norman P. Goldhawk. New York: Harper & Row, 1961. Originally published in 1952 by Macmillan Co. A theological analysis of commonalities and conflicts between Pharisaic Judaism and early Christianity.

Cadbury, Henry J. *The Peril of Modernizing Jesus.* New York: Macmillan Co., 1937. A plea to see Jesus as a Jew of the first century and not the twentieth, and the Jewishness of the Gospels.

Cohen, Arthur A. *The Myth of the Judeo-Christian Tradition.* New York: Harper & Row, 1970. Author contends not only that there is no Judeo-Christian tradition but there is in fact theological enmity between Judaism and Christianity. The so-called Judeo-Christian tradition is a myth produced by Christian guilt and Jewish neurasthenia to obscure the basic fact that Christians and Jews, to the extent that they are seriously Christians and Jews, are theological enemies.

Cohen, Martin A., ed. *The Jewish Experience in Latin America.* 2 vols. New York: KTAV, 1971. Selected studies on Latin American Jewish history from sixty volumes of the *Jewish Quarterly* and Publications of the American Jewish Historical Society, including a comprehensive introduction, bibliography, and index. A valuable source book.

Cohn, Haim. *The Trial and Death of Jesus.* New York: Harper & Row, 1971. A justice of the Supreme Court of Israel challenges certain alleged facts and interpretations of Jesus' trial and death as given in the New Testament.

Cournos, John. *An Open Letter to Jews and Christians.* New York: Oxford University Press, 1938. An examination of Jewish interpretation of Jesus and Jesus in relation to Jews in the twentieth century; a plea to Jews and Christians to join hands in the foundation of a spiritual kingdom based on freedom and love.

Dalmon, Gustaf. *Jesus-Jeshua: Studies in the Gospels.* Translated by Paul P. Levertaff. New York: KTAV Publishing House, 1971. The author, a Jewish authority on Aramaic and on early Rabbinic theology, attempts to illuminate the Jewish background and environment of Jesus, and show how Jesus' thoughts and words were the products of the people from whom he came—and with whom he also differed; a comparison of Jewish literature with the Gospels and writings of the early church.

Danby, Herbert. *The Jew and Christianity: Some Phases, Ancient and Modern, of the Jewish Attitude Towards Christianity.* New York: Macmillan Co., 1927. Originally delivered as Chapman Lectures at Sion College, London, these published lectures are a historical review of Jewish attitudes toward and relations with Christianity.

Daniélou, Jean, J.S. *Dialogue With Israel.* With a response by Rabbi Jacob B. Agus. Baltimore, Md.: Helicon Press, 1968. An investigation and an exploration of the relations between Judaism and early Christianity and their later mysticism and metaphysics. The author deplores the division within the Israel of God which has done so much harm to both Jews and Christians.

Daube, David. *The New Testament and Rabbinic Judaism.* London: University of London, 1956. An examination of old and new problems relating to the Rabbinic background of the New Testament, as suggested by parallel and quasi-parallel passages.

Davies, William David. *Christian Origins and Judaism.* Philadelphia: Westminster Press. 1962. A "study of Christianity's origins within Judaism as an integral part of the ancient Roman-Greco-Oriental world." The author urges "deeper attention to the roots of Jesus in His own times."

—————. *Paul and Rabbinic Judaism.* New York: Macmillan Co., 1955. A survey of relevant literature on the subject: a profound study of the original documents, both Christian and Jewish, to show that despite Paul's mission to the Gentiles, he remained as far as possible a Hebrew to the Hebrews and baptized his Rabbinic heritage in Christ.

Davies, Alan T. *Anti-Semitism and the Christian Mind: The Crisis of Conscience After Auschwitz.* New York: Herder and Herder, 1969. An incisive critique of post-Auschwitz Catholic and Protestant theology as it relates to Judaism; concludes with some theological guidelines for the future of Jewish-Christian relations.

Davis, Moshe, ed. *Israel: Its Role in Civilization.* New York: Harper and Brothers, 1956. "For the world Jewish community ... Israel is both reality and symbol." Modern Israel, *Eretz Yisrael,* is "in every sense, the creation of the entire Jewish people of all generations." Includes four basic themes: Israel in the perspective of the world scene, what modern scholarship teaches about ancient *Eretz Yisrael,* inner life in the State of Israel, and the nature of the interrelationship between Israel and America.

Eckardt, A. Roy. *Christianity and the Children of Israel.* New York: King's Crown Press, 1948. A theological rationale, in the light of Protestant neo-Reformation thought, for a Christian's finding a way of meaningful relationship for living with his Jewish brothers; a Christian interpretation of normative Jewish-Christian relations.

——————. *Elder and Younger Brothers: The Encounter of Jews and Christians.* New York: Charles Scribner's Sons, 1967. Examines the theological implications of the role of Jews as the consenting people in the unbroken covenant God has made with Israel and shows that the messiahship of Jesus is both grounded in and yet discontinuous with the salvation-history of Israel; presents major arguments of continuity and discontinuity between Judaism and the Christian faith.

—————— and Alice Eckardt. *Encounter With Israel: A Challenge to Conscience.* New York: Association Press, 1970. A major work on the State of Israel viewed from the perspective of its historical roots. the life of Israelis today, and recent events which challenge the world's conscience. The authors' avowed purpose is "to foster understanding of today's Israel and her people and to contribute to responsible moral and political decisions respecting that country and her place in the Middle East."

Eller, Meredith Freeman. *The Beginnings of the Christian Religion: A Guide to the History and Literature of Judaism and Christianity.* New York: Bookman Associates, 1958.

Enslin, Morton Scott. *Christian Beginnings.* New York: Harper and Row, 1938. A positive and sympathetic account of the Jewish background of the New Testament.

Epstein, Benjamin R. and Arnold Forster. *"Some of My Best Friends . . ."* New York: Farrar, Straus and Cudahy, 1962. The title of this book refers to a phrase which all too often becomes an apology and an excuse—often a smokescreen—for the discrimination used to deprive Jews of their rights and a manifestation of anti-Semitism which remains deeply imbedded in the American psyche. "One aspect of anti-Semitism—discrimination against Jews in the United States—has assumed patterns and practices that exist nowhere else in the world, making it almost a uniquely American phenomenon."

Faulhaber, Michael Von. *Judaism, Christianity and Germany.* Translated by George D. Smith. New York: Macmillan Co., 1934. Advent sermons preached in St. Michael's Church in Munich in 1933 by a Roman Catholic cardinal.

Flannery, Edward H. *The Anguish of the Jews: Twenty-Three Centuries of Anti-Semitism.* New York: Macmillan Co., 1965. The first book written by a Catholic priest on twenty-three centuries of anti-Semitism, it begins with Greek and Egyptian attitudes that formed the base root for much of what followed during the Christian era; it is a painstaking account of the guilt that casts its shadow over many, if not all, of Western Civilization's proudest accomplishments.

Foerster, Friedrick Wilhelm. *The Jews.* New York: Farrar, Straus and Co., 1961. With an introduction by Robert McAfee Brown. Originally published in Germany in 1959 as *Die Judische Frage.* The author, one of the first German Lutherans to see the anti-Semitic bias in Nazism, wrote this volume as a "token of personal gratitude for all that Christianity has received from Judaism" and as "an expression of protest against the quite amazing ingratitude which all too great a part of non-Jewish humanity has displayed towards Jewry. May this work of mine be regarded as an attempt at spiritual reparation for the indescribable wrong suffered by the Jewish people. . . ."

Fox, Gresham George. *Jesus, Pilate and Paul: An Amazingly New*

Interpretation of the Trial of Jesus Under Pontius Pilate.
Chicago: Isaacs, 1955. A study of the trial of Jesus under Pilate
and with a study of little known facts in the life of Paul before
his conversion.

Friedman, Philip. *Their Brothers' Keepers.* New York: Crown
Publishers, 1957. A study of the period during World War II,
1939-1945, and the assistance given to Jewish refugees.

Friedlander, Gerald. *The Jewish Sources of the Sermon on the
Mount.* New York: KTAV Publishing House, 1969. Originally
published in 1911. A polemical treatise intended to show
Jewish theologians how to defend Judaism and how to answer
the Christian theologians who mentioned that the teachings of
Jesus as given in the Sermon on the Mount are superior to
earlier Judaism.

Gavin, F. *The Jewish Antecedents of the Christian Sacraments.* New
York: KTAV, 1928. Presents evidence of Jewish influences on
sacramentalism associated with early strata of New Testament
literature.

Gilbert, Arthur. *A Jew in Christian America.* New York: Sheed and
Ward, 1966. A collection of essays, most all of them published
previously and written in a popular vein, by a Jewish rabbi who
has been for some years actually involved in Jewish-Christian
dialogue through his work with the Anti-Defamation League
and the National Conference of Christians and Jews.

Gillet, Lev, ed. *Judaism and Christianity.* London: J. B. Shears and
Son, 1939. Essays presented to Paul P. Levertoff.

—————. *"Communion in the Messiah": Studies in the Relationship Between Judaism and Christianity.* London: Lutterworth
Press, 1942.

Glock, Charles Y. and Rodney Stark. *Christian Beliefs and Anti-
Semitism.* New York: Harper and Row, 1966. Shows how
contemporary Christianity has shaped attitudes toward the
Jews; a sociological survey of the "religious roots of anti-
Semitism." The first volume in the Harper series based on the
University of California Five-Year Study of Anti-Semitism in
the United States, being conducted by the Survey Research
Center under a grant from the Anti-Defamation League of B'nai
B'rith.

Goldstein, Morris. *Jesus in the Jewish Tradition.* New York:
Macmillan Co., 1950. An examination of Jesus in Rabbinic

Judaism, and of Jewish literary sources, particularly Talmudic writings, which pertain to Jesus, his life, and influence.

Goodman, Paul. *The Synagogue and the Church: A Contribution to the Apologetics of Judaism.* New York: E. P. Dutton Sons, 1908.

Goppelt, Leonhard. *Jesus, Paul and Judaism: An Introduction to New Testament Theology.* New York: Thomas Nelson & Sons, 1964. A study of the context of Judaism out of which Jesus and Paul came. This volume is an English translation of the first half of *Christentum und Judentum im ersten und Zweiten Jahrhundert.*

Gordis, Robert. *Judaism in a Christian World.* New York: McGraw-Hill Book Co., 1966. A study of twentieth-century Judaism in a predominantly Christian culture.

—————. *The Root and the Branch: Judaism and the Free Society.* Chicago: University of Chicago Press, 1962. A study of the insights of the Jewish tradition in regard to intergroup relations, church and state, education, politics, and international affairs.

Graeber, Isacque and S. H. Britt, eds. *Jews in the Gentile World: The Problem of Anti-Semitism.* New York: Macmillan Co., 1942. A collection of essays by various authors on Jews in a non-Jewish environment.

Grant, Frederick C. *Ancient Judaism and the New Testament.* New York: Macmillan Co., 1959. An examination of the Jewish orientation of the New Testament from which the author concludes that "one cannot truly understand the New Testament or the religion it enshrines without a deep and sympathetic understanding of Judaism."

Grayzel, Solomon. *The Church and the Jews in the Thirteenth Century.* Rev. ed. Philadelphia: Herman Press, 1966. Originally published in 1933, this is an authoritative study by a Jewish scholar of the relations between the Roman Catholic Church and the Jews during the years 1198-1254, based on the papal letters and conciliar decrees of the period; includes texts and translations of papal letters and conciliar decrees.

Guignebert, C. A. H. *The Jewish World in the Time of Jesus.* London: Kegan Paul, Trench, Trubner, 1939. Originally published in French in 1935; reprinted in 1959 by University Books. Attempts to show that Jesus "is plainly inexplicable except as the product of his environment." Jesus was the natural product of his environment. He "was born among Jews on Jewish soil, and his message was for Jews alone. In its origin, therefore, and insofar as it is dependent on its traditional founder, Christianity must be considered a Jewish phenomenon."

Guilding, Aileen. *The Fourth Gospel and Jewish Worship: A Study of the Relation of St. John's Gospel to the Ancient Jewish Lectionary System.* Oxford: Clarendon Press, 1960. The author finds the starting point for the interpretation of the Fourth Gospel in first-century Jewish synagogue worship. The Fourth Gospel is to be seen as a Christian commentary on Old Testament lectionary readings as they were arranged for the ancient synagogue in a triennial cycle—a cycle which was already firmly established in Palestine well before the first century.

Harshbarger, Luther H. and John A. Maurant. *Judaism and Christianity: Perspectives and Traditions.* Boston: Allyn and Bacon, Inc., 1968. The subject is treated comparatively in a historical context.

Hauer, Christian E., Jr. *Crisis and Conscience in the Middle East.* Chicago: Quadrangle Books, 1970. A pro-Israel appeal to the world's conscience for resolving the Middle East crisis—a crisis which the author maintains is to be seen as a moral problem. Therefore "an immoral solution does not suffice," and "just any solution will not do"; a just and honorable settlement is needed for both sides and "is the only kind that can last and promise a bright future for Arab or Jew."

Hay, Malcom. *Foot of Pride: The Pressure of Christendom on the People of Israel for 1900 Years.* Boston: Beacon Press, 1950. Republished in 1960 as *Europe and the Jews.* A history of anti-Semitism in Christian Europe from the time of John Chrysostom in the fourth century through the Hitler Holocaust and the establishment of the State of Israel. "A book he felt had to be done, and done by a Christian; a book admitting, exposing, examining, analyzing and condemning the 'chain of error' in Christian theology and Christian ethics which is called anti-Semitism."—From the Introduction by Thomas Sugrue.

Hedenquist, Göte, ed. *The Church and the Jewish People.* London: Edinburgh House Press, 1954. A volume resulting from the need expressed by the World Council of Churches at Amsterdam for a "more detailed study" of relations between Christians and Jews. Contributors include Hans-Joachim Schoeps, Hans Kosmala, Leo Baeck, Stephen Neill, Göte Hedenquist, et al.

Heer, Friedrich. *God's First Love: Christians and Jews over Two Thousand Years.* Translated by Geoffrey Skelton. New York: Weybright and Talley, 1970. A major and poignant review of Christian anti-Semitism from New Testament times to the present.

Herberg, Will. *Protestant, Catholic, Jew: An Essay in American Religious Sociology.* Rev. ed. Garden City, N.Y.: Doubleday and Co., 1960. Descriptive of the modern American scene; a major sociological study of the interrelationship of Protestant, Catholic, and Jew in American life.

Herford, Robert Travers. *Christianity in Talmud and Midrash.* London: Williams and Norgate, 1903. Reprinted in 1966 by Reference Book Publishers, Inc. in *Library of Religious and Philosophic Thought.* An investigation by a Christian scholar into Rabbinical literature bearing upon the origin and early history of Christianity.

——————. *Judaism in the New Testament Period.* London: Lindsey Press, 1928. A study of the impact of Judaism on Christianity and Christianity upon Judaism during the New Testament period and the separation of Christianity from Judaism.

Hertzberg, Arthur. *The French Enlightenment and the Jews.* New York: Columbia University Press, 1968. A major historical study of the significance of the decrees following the French Revolution calling for the emancipation of the Jews, 28 January 1790 and 27 September 1791, whereby "for the first time in the modern history of the West all the Jews within the borders of a European state were united with all of its other citizens as equals before the law." Thus a new era in Jewish history began in France and indeed in Europe.

Isaac, Jules. *Has Anti-Semitism Roots in Christianity?* New York: National Council of Christians and Jews, 1961. Provides an emphatic, affirmative answer to the question.

——————. *Jesus and Israel.* New York: Holt, Rinehart and Winston, 1971. Edited and with a Foreword by Claire Huchet Bishop. Originally published in Paris in 1948, this volume, by a

French Jewish scholar, reflects much sympathy for Jesus as a person but recounts the contempt and social debasement of the Jews fostered by Christianity.

—————. *The Teaching of Contempt: Christian Roots of Anti-Semitism*. Translated by Helen Weaver. New York: Holt, Rinehart and Winston, 1964. An incisive analysis of the Christian roots of anti-Semitism by a French Jewish historian; includes a summary statement of the author's *Jésus et Israel*.

Jocz, Jakób. *Christians and Jews: Encounter and Mission*. London: S.P.C.K., 1966. The author, a Hebrew Christian, maintains that "the Church in her encounter with Judaism is pressed into a position in which her missionary seriousness becomes the test of her Christianity." In confrontation with the Synagogue "she can be the Church only if she is whole-heartedly a missionary Church," and "only by facing the Synagogue can the Church rediscover her true nature."

—————. *The Jewish People and Jesus Christ: A Study in the Relationship Between the Jewish People and Jesus Christ*. London: S.P.C.K., 1949. A study of the history of the relations between the Christian church and the Jews.

—————. *A Theology of Election: Israel and the Church*. New York: Macmillan Co., 1958. An examination of the theological and spiritual basis for Jewish-Christian relations seen in terms of "election"—the election of Israel and the election of the church; considers in what sense the church is Israel and, at the same time, the permanent significance of the Jewish people as marked by Israel's election.

Judaism and Christianity. New York: KTAV Publishing House, Inc., 1969, with a Prolegomenon by Ellis Rivkin. Originally published in separate volumes, 1937-1938: Vol. 1, *The Age of Transition*, edited by W. O. E. Oesterly; Vol. 2, *The Contact of Pharisaism with Other Cultures*, edited by Herbert Loewe; and Vol. 3, *Law and Religion*, edited by Erwin I. J. Rosenthal. These volumes attempt to scrutinize critically Pharisaism and the sources that undergird both Judaism and Christianity. A remarkable pioneer effort to foster Jewish-Christian scholarly endeavor in a genuinely ecumenical spirit.

Kagan, Henry Enoch. *Changing the Attitude of Christian Toward Jew*. New York: Columbia University Press, 1952. A psychological approach through religion; originally submitted as a thesis to Columbia University.

Katz, Jacob. *Exclusiveness and Tolerance: Studies in Jewish-Gentile Relations in Medieval and Modern Times.* London: Oxford Univeristy Press, 1961. A scholarly treatment of the changing attitudes of Ashkenazis Jewry towards their non-Jewish environment from the Middle Ages to the eighteenth century.

Kisch, Guido. *The Jews in Medieval Germany.* Chicago: University Press, 1949. A study of their legal and social status.

Klausner, Joseph. *From Jesus to Paul.* Translated by W. F. Stinespring. New York: Macmillan Co., 1943. Boston: Beacon Press, 1960. A study of the rise of Christianity against the background of the pagan and Jewish thought of the time in which both the common grounds of Judaism and Christianity and the issues which divide them are delineated.

——————. *Jesus of Nazareth.* Translated by Herbert Danby. New York: Macmillan Co., 1925. Numerous reprintings. A noted Jewish scholar's account of the life of Jesus in the light of the historical, religious, and socio-religious background of this time, as found in Rabbinic and Talmudic sources. Klausner concludes that the non-national character of the teachings of Jesus "inevitably brought it to pass that his people, Israel, rejected him."

Knight, George A. F., ed. *Jews and Christians: Preparation for Dialogue.* Philadelphia: Westminster Press, 1965. Attempts to help Christians understand the common ground and the differences between the two faiths, to encourage honest, searching dialogue, to help prepare the church for such dialogue, to furnish resource materials for discussion, and to raise the questions significant for such a dialogue.

Kosmala, Hans and Robert Smith. *The Jew in the Christian World.* London: Student Christian Movement Press; New York: Macmillan Co., 1942.

Lapide, Pinchas E. *Three Popes and the Jews.* New York: Hawthorne Books, Inc., 1967. A vigorous defense by an Israeli of Pope Pius XI, Pope Pius XII, and Pope John XXIII for their efforts to defend the Jews from the Nazi Holocaust and how John XXIII, "more than all other popes worked to erase the shameful Catholic position on the Jewish question."

Lay, Thomas, S.J., ed. *Jewish-Christian Relations.* St. Mary's, Kansas: St. Mary's College, 1965. Published papers of an Institute on

Jewish-Christian Relations held at St. Mary's College, St. Mary's, Kansas, 21-22 February 1965. Contributors include Jakob J. Petuchowski, Marc H. Tanenbaum, Morris Margolies, Elbert L. Spinsley, and David Rabinovitz.

Lehman, Ruth. *Nova Bibliotheca Anglo-Judaica: A Bibliographical Guide to Anglo-Jewish History, 1937-1960.* London: Jewish Historical Society of England, 1961. Prepared to bring up to date Cecil Roth's *Magna Bibliotheca Anglo-Judaica.*

Loewenstein, Rudolph M. *Christians and Jews: A Psychoanalytic Study.* Translated by Vera Damman. New York: Dell Publishing Co., 1963. Originally published in 1951. A psychoanalytic study of the causes and effects of anti-Semitism in which the author maintains that "the historical role of Israel in the birth of Christianity was the mainspring of all anti-Semitic feelings." This volume is "dedicated to the Christians who gave their lives for persecuted Jews."

Long, J. Bruce, ed. *Judaism and the Christian Seminary Curriculum.* Chicago: Loyola University Press, 1966. Published papers presented at a Catholic-Protestant Conference on Judaism and the Christian Seminary Curriculum, 24-25 March 1965, at the University of Chicago in an effort to enhance Jewish-Christian relations through a study of the Christian seminary curriculum as to its strengths and weaknesses in this area.

Lowenthal, Marvin. *The Jews of Germany.* New York: Longmans, Green and Co., 1936. A history of sixteen centuries of Jews and Jewish persecutions in Germany.

Marcus, Jacob Rader. *The Jew in the Medieval World: A Source Book, 315-1791.* New York: Temple Books, 1969. Originally published by the Jewish Publication Society. The inner life of the Jews as well as their relationship with the state and other religions; thoroughly documented.

Maritain, Jacques. *A Christian Looks at the Jewish Question.* New York: Longmans, Green, & Co., 1939.

Martin, Malachi. *The Encounter.* New York: Farrar, Straus and Giroux, 1969. Why the major religions—Christianity, Judaism, and Islam—are in crisis, and how they have failed modern man.

Moehlman, Conrad H. *The Christian-Jewish Tragedy: A Study in Religious Prejudice.* Rochester: Leo Hart, 1933. Written by a church historian as a Christian apology to Judaism for nineteen centuries of "brutal and outrageous persecution of the Jew." A summons to Christian confession for Christianity's treatment of the Jews.

Montefiore, C. G. *Rabbinic Literature and Gospel Teachings.* New York: KTAV Publishing House, 1970. First published in 1930. An examination of Rabbinic parallels to the Gospels from the perspective of Liberal Judaism. This reissue makes readily available to students of Rabbinic and New Testament literature a wealth of Talmudic and Midrashic material, learned analyses, in the light of extant scholarly literature, of many of the "religious and ethical" teachings of the Gospels and Rabbinic Judaism, as well as a corrective of the view of Rabbinic Judaism prevalent among Christian scholars of the nineteenth and twentieth centuries.

Moore, George Foot. *Judaism in the First Centuries of the Christian Era.* 3 vols. Cambridge: Harvard University Press, 1927-1930. Recently republished in two-volume paperback by Schocken. "The aim of the present work is to exhibit the religious conceptions and moral principles of Judaism, its modes of worship and observance, and its distinctive piety, in the form in which, by the end of the second century, they attained general acceptance and authority." Volume 3 is devoted to "Longer Notes and Discussions."

Neusner, Jacob, trans. *Aphrahat and Judaism: The Christian-Jewish Argument in Fourth-Century Iran.* Leiden: E. J. Brill, 1971. Contains the writings of Aphrahat, or Aphraates, relevant to Judaism and the Jews, by one of the first great fathers of the Syriac speaking church in Iran (c. 300-350); the only important written evidence on the state of the Mesopotamian-Babylonian Talmud in Sasanian times outside of the Babylonian Talmud.

Oesterreicher, John M., ed. *The Bridge: Judaeo-Christian Studies.* 5 vols. New York: Pantheon Books, 1955-1970. A Roman Catholic Series published as a yearbook of Jewish-Christian studies by the Institute for Judaeo-Christian Studies, Seton Hall University.

──────────, ed. *Brothers in Hope.* The Bridge: Judaeo-Christian Studies, vol. 5. New York: Herder and Herder, 1970. In this volume Jewish as well as Catholic scholars probe the implications of the Conciliar Statement on the Jews. Without attempting to provide any final "answer," the volume attempts to explore the meaning and significance of the Jew as a brother, not an *Unmensch* or one accursed.

Olson, Bernhard E. *Faiths and Prejudice: Intergroup Problems in Protestant Curricula.* New Haven: Yale University Press, 1963. Reports the findings and insights derived from a massive Protestant self-study, carried out by the author (a Methodist minister) over a seven-year period at the Yale Divinity School, to determine whether religious education is a possible breeding ground for prejudice; shows what church publications are saying about the religious communities, especially the Jewish. The most systematic and thorough of its kind ever undertaken.

Parkes, James William. *Antisemitism: A Concise World-History.* Chicago: Quadrangle Books, 1969. First published in 1963. A distinguished authority on the relationship between Jews and non-Jews discusses anti-Semitism as a modern phenomenon and traces it through the nineteenth century to its historic roots in the early Christian church; includes a significant chapter on anti-Semitism in the Soviet Union and an important chapter on the State of Israel's relation to the Arabs. The author is in many ways *the* Christian pioneer in Jewish-Christian relations in the modern world.

————. *The Conflict of the Church and the Synagogue: A Study in the Origins of Anti-Semitism.* New York: Meridian Books, 1961. Originally published in 1934 by Soncino Press. A classic study of anti-Semitism which addresses itself to the question: "Why was there a medieval ghetto?" Traces the status of the Jews in the Roman world and Jewish relations with pagans and Christians through the early Middle Ages.

————. *The Emergence of the Jewish Problem, 1878-1939.* Oxford: Oxford University Press, 1946.

————. *An Enemy of the People: Anti-Semitism.* New York: Penguin Books, 1946.

————. *The Foundations of Judaism and Christianity.* Chicago: Quadrangle Books, 1960. A Christian scholar pleads with great sympathy for a mutual understanding between Jews and Christians, and presents here, based upon thorough research, the common foundations of these two great faiths. The book is divided in three parts: "The Common Foundation," "The

Emergence of Christianity," and "The Emergence of Rabbinic Judaism."

——————. *The Jewish Problem in the Modern World.* Oxford: Oxford University Press, 1946. Based on an English edition published in 1939, this up-dated edition is divided into three parts: "The World Before 1914," "1919-1939," and "The Second World War," which recounts the disaster in Europe and Palestine, 1939-1945.

——————. *Judaism and Christianity.* Chicago: University of Chicago Press, 1948. Based on the Charles William Eliot Lectures at the Jewish Institute of Religion, New York City, 1946-1947.

——————. *Prelude to Dialogue: Jewish-Christian Relationships.* New York: Schocken Books, Inc., 1969. A selection of some of the most scholarly and important lectures given by a Christian scholar who is probably the world's foremost non-Jewish authority on Jewish affairs and Jewish-Christian relations. These essays explore the symbiosis of Judaism and Christianity through historical analysis.

Patai, Raphael. *Israel Between East and West: A Study in Human Relations.* Philadelphia: Jewish Publication Society of America, 1953.

Pinson, Koppel, ed. *Essays on Antisemitism.* 2d ed., rev. and enl. New York: Conference on Jewish Relations, 1946. Essays intended to promote understanding of the history and psychology of anti-Semitism by both Jews and non-Jews; written with care and considerable documentation by outstanding scholars including: Hannah Arendt, Solomon Grayzel, Waldemar Gurian, Jacob R. Marcus, Samuel Rosenblatt, Mark Vishniak, et al.

Poliakov, Leon. *The History of Anti-Semitism.* Translated by Richard Howard. New York: Vanguard Press, 1965. Originally published in France in 1955. A review of anti-Semitism from the time of Jesus to the present.

Richardson, Peter. *Israel in the Apostolic Church.* Cambridge: Cambridge University Press, 1969. Author maintains that Justin represents the culmination of estrangement of the early church from Judaism, a development in which the church increasingly

viewed itself as "the heir of all of which Israel once possessed."
Traces the development in the patristic writings and, book by
book, within the New Testament itself.

Rollins, E. William and Harry Zohn, eds. *Men of Dialogue: Martin
Buber and Albrecht Goes.* New York: Funk and Wagnalls, 1969.
A moving account of dialogue between, and collection of
writings by, perhaps the most important Jewish thinker of the
twentieth century and a former Christian chaplain in Hitler's
army.

Rosenberg, Stuart E. *Bridge to Brotherhood: Judaism's Dialogue
With Christianity.* New York: Abelard-Schuman, 1961. An
introduction to Judaism, written by a Jewish scholar, to enable
Christians to better understand Judaism. An authentic contribution to Jewish-Christian dialogue. The four parts of this volume
include: "Sacred Places," "Sacred Moments," "Sacred Times
and Seasons," and "Sacred Ideas."

Rosenstock-Huessy, Eugen, ed. *Judaism Despite Christianity.*
University: Univeristy of Alabama Press, 1969. Contains the
"Letters on Christianity and Judaism" between Eugen
Rosenstock-Huessy and Franz Rosenzweig, written in 1916,
along with an important introductory chapter by Harold
Stahmer and essays by Alexander Altman and Dorothy Emmet.

Rosenzweig, Franz. *The Star of Redemption.* Translated by William
H. Hallo. New York: Holt, Rinehart and Winston, 1971.
Originally published in Germany in 1921, this translation is
based on the 1930 edition of *Stern der Erlösung.* After seriously
considering conversion to Christianity, the author experienced a
profound "closeness to God" in a traditional synagogue Yom
Kippur service in Berlin in 1913, which led him to an
affirmation of his Jewish faith and his presentation of Judaism
and Christianity "as equally 'true' and valid views of reality."
The author has been called "the single greatest influence on the
religious thought of North American Jewry" and this book has
been described as "the most significant contribution to Jewish
theology in the twentieth century." Contains numerous and
extended references to Jesus, Christianity, and the church.

Rotenstreich, Nathan. *The Recurring Pattern: Studies in Anti-
Judaism in Modern Thought.* New York: Horizon Press, 1964.

Roth, Cecil. *The Jews in the Renaissance.* Philadelphia: The Jewish Publication Society of America, 1959. An important study of the significant role played by the Jews, and especially by Italian Jewry, in the Renaissance, particularly before the fifteenth century.

——————. *Magna Bibliotheca Anglo-Judaica: A Bibliographical Guide to Anglo-Jewish History.* London: The Jewish Historical Society of England, University College, 1937. Definitive.

Rowley, Harold Henry. *The Servant of the Lord, and Other Essays on the Old Testament.* 2d ed. Oxford: Basil Blackwell, 1965. Originally published in 1952. A major contribution to Jewish-Christian dialogue of the Servant of the Lord motif as well as many of other Biblical themes in the light of Jewish and Christian scholarship.

Runes, Dagobert D. *The Jew and the Cross.* New York: Philosophical Library. 1965. A bitter and scathing indictment of Church Christianity for giving birth and sustained support to anti-Semitism.

Sandmel, Samuel. *The First Christian Century in Judaism and Christianity: Certainties and Uncertainties.* New York: Oxford University Press, 1969. Deals with the first century from the perspective of a historian of religion, not as a theologian, by a Jewish scholar who is a New Testament specialist; the author summarizes his own views on the chief issues in New Testament scholarship.

——————. *The Genius of Paul—A Study in History.* New York: Farrar, Straus and Giroux, 1958. A study by a Jewish scholar of Paul's teachings in the light of his Jewish background.

——————. *A Jewish Understanding of the New Testament.* New York: Hebrew Union College Press, 1956. New York: University, 1960. A major study of the literature of the New Testament by an outstanding Jewish scholar, preceded by an analysis of the historical circumstances and background of the era; concludes with a section devoted to the significance of the New Testament.

——————. *The Several Israels.* New York: KTAV, 1971. An examination of the doctrine of the Chosen as a source of exclusiveness and universalism, reflected in claimants to the title of the True Israel from the descendants of Abraham, the inhabitants of the Promised Land, to the Christian sects (including the Puritan settlers of New England). Chapter headings include "The Hebrew Israel," "The Christian's Israel," "The State of Israel," and "The True Israel."

——————. *We Jews and Jesus.* New York: Oxford University Press, 1965. An informed treatise on the what and why of the Jewish attitude toward Jesus.

——————. *We Jews and You Christians: An Inquiry into Attitudes.* New York: J. B. Lippencott Co., 1967. A personal statement by a distinguished Jewish scholar who attempts to reflect, in the absence of any central Jewish authority, the attitudes of Jews toward Christians, both collectively and individually. In response to the Vatican Council's *Declaration on the Jews,* the author offers a proposed Jewish declaration on the Christians: "The Synagogue and the Christian People."

Scharper, Philip, ed. *Torah and Gospel: Jewish and Catholic Theology in Dialogue.* New York: Sheed and Ward, 1966. Shows that the relation between Jew and Christian cannot remain merely on the social level but must meet on the plane of theological confrontation of Torah and Gospel.

Schneider, Peter. *The Dialogue of Christians and Jews.* New York: Seabury Press, 1966. Shows how much Christians and Jews could learn from each other in a dialogue freed from misunderstandings of the past.

Schoeps, Hans-Joachim. *The Jewish-Christian Argument: A History of Theologies in Conflict.* 3d ed. New York: Holt, Rinehart and Winston, Inc., 1963. An excellent account of the theological controversies of Judaism and Christianity, from those of the Church Fathers and the Rabbis of the early Talmudic period through the first half of the twentieth century.

——————. *Jewish Christianity: Factional Disputes in the Early Church.* Philadelphia: Fortress Press, 1969. An important introduction to a little known sect within early Christianity known as the Ebionites, whose theology attempted to bridge the gulf between Judaism and Christianity.

——————. *The Theology of the Apostle in the Light of Jewish Religious History.* Philadelphia: Westminster Press, 1961. A comprehensive, scholarly study of Pauline theology by a Jew "who also wishes to do justice to the Judaism, whence Paul sprang," and in the light of which Pauline theology is to be interpreted and even Pauline Christological thought is to be understood.

Selznick, Gertrude J. and Stephen Steinberg. *The Tenacity of Prejudice: Anti-Semitism in Contemporary America.* New York: Harper and Row, 1969. Part I measures the extent of contemporary anti-Semitism and is largely descriptive. Part II identifies the social and demographic strata in which anti-Semitism is most prevalent, and is largely analytical. Part III, interpretive in character, seeks to understand why anti-Semitism is more likely to be found among some kinds of individuals than among others.

Silver, A. H. *Where Judaism Differed: An Inquiry into the Distinctiveness of Judaism.* Philadelphia: Jewish Publication Society, 1957.

Stendahl, Krister, ed. *The Scrolls and the New Testament.* New York: Harper and Brothers, 1957. A mature summation of the significance of the Dead Sea Scrolls, Qumran texts, for research into the beginnings of Christianity and their relationship to the New Testament.

Schweitzer, Frederick M. *A History of the Jews since the First Century A.D.* New York: Macmillan Co., 1971. Written by a Roman Catholic, this work attempts a detached view of Jewish-Christian relations as a corrective to the centuries of Christian scholars' neglect and distortion of Jewish history; a fresh re-examination of Jewish history in the light of Vatican II and its "Declaration on the Relationship of the Church to Non-Christian Religions" and the ecumenical climate of today.

Swidler, Leonard J., ed. *Scripture and Ecumenism: Protestant, Catholic, Orthodox, and Jewish.* Duquesne University Studies, Theological Series. Pittsburg: Duquesne University Press, 1965. Papers delivered at an ecumenical seminar held at Duquesne University, Spring 1964. Includes a paper on "Judaism, Scriptures, and Ecumenism," by Steven S. Schwarzschild, a Jewish scholar.

Synan, Edward A. *The Popes and the Jews in the Middle Ages.* New York: Macmillan Co., 1965. Published under the sponsorship of the Institute of Judaeo-Christian Studies of Seton Hall, this volume is an examination of medieval documents directly bearing upon Jewish-papal relations. All texts cited are freshly translated for this study. The last chapter contains reflections

on the significance of what the documents have to tell
Christians today. A valuable study.

Toynbee, Arnold, ed. *The Crucible of Christianity: Judaism,
Hellenism, and the Historical Background of the Christian
Faith.* New York: World Publishing Co., 1969. A magnificent
volume on the background of Christianity. Note especially
chaps. 1-3, pp. 9-98 and chap. 12, pp. 283-298 for relationship
of Christianity to Judaism.

Tractenberg, Joshua. *The Devil and the Jews: The Medieval
Conception of the Jew and Its Relation to Modern Anti-
Semitism.* New Haven: Yale University Press, 1943. Reprinted
by Harper & Row in 1966. An important study of the medieval
concept of the Jew and its bearing on the question: "How is it
that men believe of the Jews what common sense would forbid
them to believe of anyone else?" The volume is divided into
three parts: "The Demonic Jew," "The Jew as Sorcerer," and
"The Jew as Heretic."

Trattner, Ernest R. *As a Jew Sees Jesus.* New York: Charles
Scribner's Sons, 1931. A work based upon the "amazing" fact
that, in the words of Emerson, "The name of Jesus is not so
much written as ploughed into the history of the world." The
author, as a Jew, cites Emerson's statement to say "nothing
quite like it has ever happened on so large a scale in the annals
of man." Among subjects treated by the author are "The
Jewishness of Jesus," "Jesus and the Pharisees," and "Jesus and
the Modern Jew."

Trepp, L. *Eternal Faith, Eternal People: A Journey into Judaism.*
Englewood Cliffs, N.J.: Prentice-Hall, 1962. An introduction to
Judaism, which includes a discussion of differences between
Judaism and Christianity.

Troki, Isaac ben Abraham. *Faith Strengthened (Chizzuk Emunah).*
Translated by Moss Mocatta. New York: KTAV, 1970. A
vigorous refutation by a distinguished Karaite scholar, a
Lithuanian Jew, of Christian polemics against Judaism. Written
nearly four centuries ago for the author's fellow Jews who were
confronted by the Christian mission to the Jews, "this book,"
as Trude Weiss-Rosmarin has written, "continues to hold a place
of importance unequaled by any other work of Jewish polemics
with Christianity."

Tumen, Melvin M. *An Inventory and Appraisal of Research on*

American Anti-Semitism. New York: Anti-Defamation League of B'nai B'rith, 1961.

Valentin, H. *Antisemitism Historically and Critically Examined.* Translated by A. G. Chater. New York: The Viking Press, 1936.

Werner, Eric. *The Sacred Bridge: The Interdependence of Liturgy and Music in Synagogue and Church During The First Millennium.* New York: Columbia University Press, 1959. The author maintains that "however far the two religions drifted apart in their tenets, a sacred bridge still spans the abyss, and allows for an exchange of views and moral concepts and, with them, of liturgical forms in which the dogmas and concepts find their way to the senses." The study is divided into two parts: "Historic-Liturgical," and "Musical Comparisons and Studies."

Wilde, Robert. *The Treatment of the Jews in the Greek Christian Writers of the First Three Centuries.* Washington: Catholic University of America Press, 1949.

Wilken, Robert L. *Judaism and the Early Christian Mind: A Study of Cyril of Alexandria's Exegesis and Theology.* New Haven: Yale University Press, 1971. An investigation of the writings of Cyril of Alexandria which reveals the crucial influence of the polemical conflicts with Judaism voiced by the early church fathers; a review of the first four centuries of Jewish-Christian relations and the influences of these relations on Cyril's exegetical writings and his theology.

Williams, Arthur L. *Talmudic Judaism and Christianity.* New York: Macmillan Co., 1933.

Winter, Paul. *On the Trial of Jesus.* Berlin: Walter D. E. Gruyter & Co., 1961. A critical evaluation by a European Jewish scholar of aspects of the Gospel accounts of the arrest, trial, and crucifixion of Jesus.

Wolfson, H. A. *Philo: Foundations of Religious Philosophy in Judaism, Christianity, and Islam.* 2 vols. Cambridge, Mass.: Harvard University Press, 1947. A scholarly treatment of the philosophy of Philo and its growth and development in the succeeding seventeen centuries, with an examination of the effect of Philonic philosophy on the religious philosophy of Judaism, Christianity, and Islam.

Yates, George A., ed. *In Spirit and in Truth: Aspects of Judaism and Christianity.* London: Hodder & Stoughton, Ltd., 1934. This volume constitutes the first Jewish-Christian symposium ever published in England. The contributors, Jewish and Christian, include: A. E. Garvie, B. H. Streeter, C. H. Montefiore, Herbert M. J. Loewe, I. I. Mattuck, John Oman, J. Abelson, H. F. Reinhart, et al. A historically significant collection of essays by distinguished scholars.

Zeitlin, S. *Who Crucified Jesus?* New York: Block Publishing Co., 1964. A historical study of the background and development of the first century of the Christian era, with focus on the trial and crucifixion of Jesus; the author maintains that neither the modern Jew nor his ancestors were responsible in any way whatsoever for the death of Jesus.

CONTRIBUTORS

A. ROY ECKARDT (B.A., Brooklyn College; B.D., Yale University; Ph.D., Columbia University; L.H.D., Hebrew Union College-Jewish Institute of Religion) is Professor of Religion and Chairman of the Department at Lehigh University. A past president of the American Academy of Religion, Dr. Eckardt served as Editor of the *Journal of the American Academy of Religion*, 1961-1969. Approximately seventy-five of his articles have been published in scholarly and professional journals. His publications include *Christianity and the Children of Israel* (1948), *The Surge of Piety in America* (1958), *Elder and Younger Brothers* (1967), *The Theologian at Work* (ed., 1970), and *Encounter With Israel* (with Alice L. Eckardt, 1970).

ROBERT T. HANDY (B.A., Brown University; B.D., Colgate-Rochester Divinity School; Ph.D., University of Chicago Divinity School) is Acting Dean and Professor of Church History at Union Theological Seminary, New York City. Dr. Handy is a former president of the American Society of Church History. A member of the Editorial Board of the Library of Christian Thought, he is co-editor of *American Christianity* (2 vols., 1960-1963) and *Theology and Church in Times of Change* (1970), editor of *The Social Gospel in America* (1966), and author of *Members One of Another* (1969) and the forthcoming *A Christian America: Protestant Hopes and Historical Realities.*

FRANKLIN H. LITTELL (B.A., Cornel College; B.D., Union Theological Seminary; Ph.D., Yale University; honors: D.D., Cornell College; Dr. Theol., University of Marburg; Grand Order of Merit of the German Federal Republic) is Professor of Religion at Temple University. A member of the Editorial Council of *Journal of Church and State*, he is a frequent contributor to numerous scholarly journals. His publications include *The Anabaptist View of the Church* (1952), *The Free Church* (1957), *The German Phoenix* (1960), *From State Church to Pluralism* (1962), *The Church and the Body Politic* (1968), and *Wild Tongues: A Handbook for Social Pathology* (1969).

SEYMOUR SIEGEL (B.A., University of Chicago; M.H.L., D.H.L., Jewish Theological Seminary of America) is Professor of Theology at the Jewish Theological Seminary of America. A Fellow of the Conference on Science, Philosophy, and Religion and of the Society for Religion in Higher Education, he is a member of the Editorial Board of the Jewish Publication Society, *Jewish Heritage, Our Age,* and *Conservative Judaism.* His articles and reviews have appeared in numerous journals. An editor of the *New Jewish Encyclopedia* now being prepared by an international team of scholars, he is co-author of *The Jewish Dietary Laws* (1960) and *A Faithful Passion: A Theology of Judaism,* soon to be published.

JAMES E. WOOD, JR. (B.A., Carson-Newman College; M.A., Columbia
    University; B.D., Th.M., Th.D., Southern Baptist Theological Seminary,
    Louisville, Kentucky) is Professor of Religion and Director of the J. M.
    Dawson Studies in Church and State at Baylor University. Editor of
    Markham Press of Baylor University, he has been Editor of *Journal of
    Church and State* since its founding in 1959. He is the author of approxi-
    mately forty-five articles in various scholarly and professional journals,
    contributor to several books, co-author of *Church and State in Scripture,
    History, and Constitutional Law* (1958), editor of *Church and State*
    (1960), author of *The Problem of Nationalism in Church-State Relation-
    ships* (1969), and the forthcoming *An Annotated Bibliography on Church
    and State.*